# GREEK LAW
## in its Political Setting

# GREEK LAW

## in its Political Setting

*Justifications not Justice*

*Edited by*
L. Foxhall *and* A.D.E. Lewis

CLARENDON PRESS · OXFORD

*This book has been printed digitally and produced in a standard specification
in order to ensure its continuing availability*

# OXFORD
UNIVERSITY PRESS

Great Clarendon Street, Oxford OX2 6DP

Oxford University Press is a department of the University of Oxford.
It furthers the University's objective of excellence in research, scholarship,
and education by publishing worldwide in

Oxford New York

Auckland Cape Town Dar es Salaam Hong Kong Karachi
Kuala Lumpur Madrid Melbourne Mexico City Nairobi
New Delhi Shanghai Taipei Toronto
With offices in
Argentina Austria Brazil Chile Czech Republic France Greece
Guatemala Hungary Italy Japan South Korea Poland Portugal
Singapore Switzerland Thailand Turkey Ukraine Vietnam

ISBN 0-19-814085-1

# Contents

# List of Figures

# Note on Citations and References

In a book which draws on a wide range of interdisciplinary scholarship, and which is itself intended to be accessible to a broad read-
ership from several backgrounds, the editors have avoided
abbreviating titles of journals and ancient sources. For ancient literary sources, full English titles have normally been used in text references. References to inscriptions have been cited as standard
Harvard-system references whenever possible. However, the standard collections of inscriptions and papyri, which form the basic
foundations for the study and use of epigraphical and papyrologi-
cal sources, and whose reference numbers uniquely identify individual inscriptions and papyri, have been cited using the normal
conventions:

IG       *Inscriptiones Graecae* (Berlin, 1873– )
SEG      *Supplementum epigraphicum Graecum*
IC       *Inscriptions Creticae*; IC IV = Guarducci (1950)
P.Oxy.   *The Oxyrhynchus Papyri* (London, 1898– )

# I

# Introduction

LIN FOXHALL AND ANDREW LEWIS

This volume examines some of the many ways in which law inte-
grated with other aspects of life in ancient Greece, and explores the
extent and the limits of that integration. The idea for the seminar
series, held at the Institute of Classical Studies in 1989, in which
this work originated, arose from our sense of discontent with the
formalist and evolutionist approaches which have played a major
part in the traditions of Greek legal studies. The papers presented
in that seminar and collected here reveal a number of different
pathways between law and political, social, and economic life in
Greek societies. Emanating from different scholarly traditions of the
study of ancient law, these papers offer a range of contrasting but
complementary insights rarely collected together. The editors, an
ancient historian with some background in anthropology and a
lawyer specializing in legal history, are eager that the volume
should communicate with readers interested in the history and
development of law from a wide range of backgrounds. To this end
we have made efforts to keep both classical quotation and legal jar-
gon to a minimum and to explain those technical terms used in the
text. For further assistance we would refer the reader to the excellent glossary in Todd (1993); there is a less full glossary in
Cartledge et al. (1990).

   To abandon formalism is not to reduce law to social history.
Indeed, it is impossible to write social history directly from law (the
recent attempts by Sealey 1990 and Just 1989 are not really successful), for law focuses on the exceptional, the difficult, and the
ambiguous parts of social life, rather than the ordinary. Cohen's
recent work (1991) admirably demonstrates the difficulties of relating lived moral systems to the legal 'rules'. Clearly he has seen the
intellectual pitfalls of trying to reconstruct social systems directly
from legal sources, and adeptly avoids them by categorizing his

work as 'an exercise in historical legal sociology' (Cohen 1991: 5), in an allusion to a modern classic of English legal positivism (Hart 1961). Surviving laws and legal information from ancient Greece, even when we possess large so-called 'codes' like the famous example from Gortyn, in fact cover only a very limited number of aspects of social, economic, and religious life (see Davies, this volume). Laws are not norms, rather they are strategies for dealing with difficult situations. *Whose* strategies, then, becomes a crucial issue.

Law in classical and archaic Greek cities appears as a set of systems that are, in certain respects, self-contained. Lawcourts have their own regulations, procedures, and even logic. Laws exist as formal and formulaic entities, whether as written texts or in other forms (see Thomas, Todd, this volume). Legal specialists are recognized (see below and Todd, this volume). Yet law and litigation in the world of the *polis* (city-state) are not nearly so self-contained, autonomous, and detached from other realms as in the industrial (even in the Roman) world. Legal language was also 'the language of the street' (Todd, this volume; Todd and Millett 1990: 17): though courtroom language often used ordinary words with context-specific technical meanings, technical terminology used exclusively in law was never developed. Lawcourts themselves were also often political bodies, for example the Athenian *boule*, 'council' (which examined officials when they finished their terms of office or held pre-trial hearings for officials accused of misbehaviour while in office), or the Areopagos (the council of ex-archons, which, among its other duties, also tried cases for homicide). Behaviour in legal actions, in court, often had ramifications for behaviour, reputations, and relationships outside the courtroom (Foxhall, this volume). In short, law in Greek cities was pre-Roman and yet not primitive. To study only the formal aspects and the procedural details of legal life in Greek cities is to miss the full impact of law and litigation within Greek societies.

This approach must necessarily side with Todd and Millett (1990: 7–11) in the long-standing debate about 'Greek law'. We agree that as a coherent entity it does not exist. Indeed, if law in Greek cities only takes on its full meaning in context, from the ways in which it interacts with other spheres of life in specific times, places, and circumstances, then resorting to a notion of 'Greek law' for explanations is unhelpful. But the structural consistency of legal behaviour within the wide range of Greek times and places covered in the papers here suggests that a notion of 'Greek law', or perhaps rather 'Greek legal behaviour', as variations on a theme does remain analytically useful (see especially Debrunner Hall, this volume; Foxhall 1989). While not thus advocating a return to the notion of 'Greek law' as explanation (Mitteis 1891), we would not dismiss it as a category of useful enquiry (cf. Finley 1986: 134-46).

A number of recent works by classical scholars have focused on law in conjunction with 'social control' and dispute settlement (Gagarin 1986; Fisher 1990, 1992; Carter 1986, Sealey 1990, Hunter 1994). Conflict may be seen in itself as a means to achieve social order (Todd and Millett 1990, following S. Roberts 1979). In so far as 'social control' provides a useful explanation for behaviour (which is debatable, see Foxhall, this volume), it frequently occurs outside legal systems in Greek cities. On the other hand, it has been convincingly argued by Todd (1993) and Todd and Millett (1990: 6-7, 16-17) that legal debate and laws in Greek cities centre almost exclusively on procedure rather than substance. The contributors to this volume would support that proposition (see Thomas, Thür, Debrunner Hall, Todd, this volume). This brings into focus a problem raised by Todd and Millett (1990: 15-16) and explored in some depth by Todd (1993): that of the close relationships between law and politics in ancient Greece. Both these works restrict the terms of the debate largely to classical Athens, though variations on the theme occurred in other Greek cities (Todd 1993: 158). In democratic Athens, as Todd (1993: 153) perceptively points out, access to the processes of law was important not only in terms of participating as a litigant but, probably more significantly for most men, in terms of participation as a 'juror' (*dikastes*). Political and social control of legal procedure (both its formulation and access to it in all senses) must therefore have been an ongoing discourse with other systems for the distribution and fragmentation of power, and these systems varied considerably among Greek city states. Here again we are back to the question of *whose* strategies, *whose* terms of argument, are represented in Greek discourses of law and political power?

For early Greece different aspects of this problem are considered here by Thomas, Thür and Davies. Davies deals with the specific example of Gortyn between the sixth and fourth centuries BC and, by a careful analysis of the laws which are not part of the 'Great Code', provides a convincing explanation for the function of the numerous inscribed laws from that city (including the 'Great Code' itself). Significantly, his explanation places these laws firmly in a *political* framework, which eliminates the necessity to explain 'codification' as a step in the evolution of 'social control'. That the overriding aim of legal codification is dispute settlement then also becomes questionable.

Similarly, Thomas's argument is that the development of a distinguishable sphere of written laws, which came to be considered 'the law' (fixed procedural rules to which anyone could refer), in Greek cities occurred over a long period. Indeed, the distinction in the fifth and fourth centuries BC between 'written' and 'unwritten' laws is only meaningful once people have become accustomed to considering written laws as 'normal', and she presents considerable evidence to show that earlier this was not so. Again, this leaves open the likelihood that 'social control' frequently happens outside the law (in so far as that is even meaningful as a separable category in early *poleis*, 'city-states'). It also cast further doubt on the idea that legal 'codification' in early Greece was the product of literacy and was stimulated by the need for increased social control and the settlement of disputes—her arguments suggest that for these purposes *written* law made little difference.

Thür's analysis of Homeric trials emphasizes the central importance of settling an issue (though not necessarily the dispute) by agreeing upon a suitable procedure for determining it, here an oath to be sworn by either party. The problem, as he makes clear, comes when an oath is technically correct, but is 'crooked' (*skolios*). That is, it is technically 'just', but the result achieved is not perceived as justice by at least one party. Here again, the spillover of grievances out of the legal sphere into the social and political is obvious—the 'bribe-eating' kings of Hesiod's *Works and Days* provide one example.

What emerges clearly is that law and the control (and use) of legal procedure in both archaic and classical Greece are not only closely linked to political power, but only take on their full meaning in a broadly political context. Political power, like so much of public life in classical Greece, is competitive and agonistic. Moreover, competition in any one of these arenas—political, social, economic, legal—has implications for the success of competitors in all of them (cf. Todd 1993: 159; E. Harris 1994, whose citation of the conflicts between Aischines and Demosthenes provides a good

Athenian example of this phenomenon). Here, Thomas's discussion (in this volume) of the powerful political roles of the officials in various cities who were responsible for remembering laws or legal judgements is important—clearly this knowledge was power. This contrasts interestingly with the very different situation in Athens at the end of the fifth century BC analysed by Todd (this volume). In this case, the codification of laws (in a sense the first proper legal codification in Athens) by an *ad hoc* board of officials can be seen to have occurred in a highly politicized setting. From the attack on one of these officials in Lysias 30 it is not easy to understand the political or social positions of the various players. But it is clear that Nikomachos (the official under fire) was accused of using his specialized knowledge illegitimately for his own personal and political ends, yet it is also implied that the possession of such specialized legal knowledge was comparable to the mastery of a mean and servile trade (and thus implied his social inferiority). Knowledge, at least in some contexts, is disrespectable power?

Competition for power and prestige is characteristic of many aspects of communal life in Greek cities, though it is best documented for classical Athens. The papers by Foxhall and Todd touch on the ways in which competition at law is part of this larger ethic of competition, which dominates most other aspects of life. From this point of view, disputes may lie in wait to be created and expanded, rather than settled, in the lawcourts (Todd 1993: 153). So, for example, Foxhall here discusses the ways in which disputes involving women may come to appear in our sources as disputes between men in the courts. She shows how events in the lawcourts (from which women were largely excluded) come in turn to affect women's lives in other contexts.

There were many areas beyond the reach of law in Greek-city states. Obviously this is true of all societies, not least our own. But the particulars of what the law touches and what it does not are revealing about the nature of Greek societies as a whole and especially in terms of how the realm of 'private life' interacts with the male 'public' and civic world (see Cohen 1991: 7097). A good example of the differences in this regard between classical Greece and other societies, both ancient and modern, is the treatment of murder as a private religious offence for which the prosecutor can only be a close relative of the victim. This has, in turn, interesting consequences for punishment (Debrunner Hall, this volume).

Todd's paper addresses the issue of professional legal specialists of the sort familiar from Roman times up to our own, who claim technical mastery of the details of written law, and who advise laymen on these technicalities. They must also have acted as guides through the complex, interlocking regulations and court procedures, for advocates appearing on behalf of clients did not exist in classical Athens, nor anywhere else in classical Greece as far as we know. The nearest we have to such characters is Nikomachos, whose very command of technicalities could be used by his opponents to cast him in an unfavourable light (see Todd, this volume). Instead, the specialists, evidence of whose work we possess in some abundance, concentrated on techniques of performance, not technicalities of law. Proof consisted of *persuasion* (and performance contributed greatly to persuasiveness), rather than precedent and strict application of regulations (Worthington 1994; E. Harris 1994). Though laws are often cited in forensic speeches, precedents are not. Even when laws are quoted, it can sometimes be shown that they are irrelevant or incorrect in the particular case (see Foxhall 1990: 94, and this volume). Truly valuable legal knowledge, then, is method, not content; procedure, not substance. The path to this knowledge is provided by élite education, particularly in rhetoric, through which the rich and powerful can appropriate the law and mobilize it as one of their political strategies, this even in democratic Athens where the masses of ordinary citizens had undoubted access to the processes of law.

What is largely absent in Greece is any sense of law as an autonomous discipline, divorced in practice from all political, religious, or social considerations. The autonomy of law, a notion which permeates modern legal systems and gives rise to such notions as the Rule of Law and the Separation of Powers, is an idea first found amongst the Romans. It is among the many aspects of the Roman legal tradition in Western thought. Itself a product of the rise in late Republican Rome of a discrete body of men with a monopoly of legal expertise which could seemingly transcend the collapsing political and social structure, the autonomy of law was fostered in the Imperial age by a government anxious to be seen to preserve Republican virtues. Whilst these jurists affected independence, they were largely dependent upon government for their political and economic advancement. This did not prevent their developing sophisticated and relatively value-free techniques of legal analysis, which contributed in large measure to form the characteristic robustness of Roman law and which served to endear it to subsequent generations. The complex story of how Roman law came to underlie most of the legal systems of Europe lies beyond the scope of these pages (for a recent collection of views see Lewis and Ibbetson 1994). It cannot be too heavily emphasized how different the legal conceptions thus generated in the modern world are from those appropriate to an understanding of classical Greece.

Of course the very characterization of legal systems as exhibiting autonomy is challenged. Autonomy grants the legal expert an apparent immunity from criticism on moral grounds and appears to privilege the system from political pressures. However central and even essential the notion of autonomy is to the workings of modern legal systems, to the lawyers' images of themselves and their function in society, it must be doubted whether such abstraction from the pressures of ordinary political life is ever achievable. The ancient Greek experience demonstrates the extent to which sophisticated social structures, and moreover ones which generated philosophical and scientific conceptions which remain at the heart of Western experience, could flourish without any such understanding of the workings of law. Law, for the Greeks, was a tool not a master.

Indeed, as Debrunner Hall points out, in classical Athens it was quite possible to be punished for an offence covered by no specific law, in part because of the wide range of available procedures under which prosecution might be made for any particular offence (Osborne 1985). In these circumstances, punishment itself, like law, is inextricably intertwined with the class, status, and economic position of the offender, as Debrunner Hall stresses. In other words, it is politized. The contrast between Debrunner Hall's paper on punishment in classical Athens and how it compares to punishment in other Greek cities, and Saunders's work on punishment for impiety in Plato's ideal state, raises many interesting questions about what Greeks thought official state punishment was. Deterrence, revenge, avoidance of pollution (essentially religious), and the preservation of household and male individual autonomy all seem to enter into ideologies of punishment (and other sanctions, see Thomas, this volume) in classical Greece. Significantly, reform of offenders has no place, except in Plato's ideal state.

Law and legal action in archaic and classical Greek cities

represent a specialized arena in which the normal conflicts and contests inherent in these societies take on particular and important forms and significance. Access to this arena was in some ways (and some times and places) quite restricted, though in others less so. A number of dynamic tensions govern the relationships between this semi-autonomous legal arena and other spheres of life. An ideology of equality before the law was juxtaposed with a practical reality of individuals' unequal abilities to cope with it. A sense of uncertainty about the roles of performer and audience, judges and contestants, seems characteristic of the Athenian courts we know best. It is hard to draw firm lines between the settlement of cases in court and the spillover of legal actions into the agora, the streets, the fields, and the houses of Attica. In these circumstances it is hardly surprising if justice gives way to justification.

# 2

# Written in Stone? Liberty, Equality, Orality and the Codification of Law[1]

## ROSALIND THOMAS

## 1. INTRODUCTION

In late fifth and fourth century Athens it was a platitude that written law brought justice for all alike, and thus that it was the basis for the democracy. As a character in Euripides' *Suppliants* says (433 f.), 'when the laws have been written down both the weak and the rich have equal justice'. Gorgias also saw written law as the guardian of justice (Diels and Kranz 1951–2: 82, fr. 11a, § 30 (*Palamedes*)). This close relation between justice, democracy, and written law was apparently confirmed still earlier by Solon's codification of the laws in writing. As he says himself in one poem, 'I wrote down laws alike for rich and poor, fitting straight justice to each' (frag. 36W = Aristotle, *Constitution of the Athenians* 12. 4). Aristotle criticized the Spartan ephors because they determined cases by their own judgement and not by written law (*kata grammata kai tous nomous*): there is an implicit comparison with the rule of law at Athens (*Politics* 1270ᵇ28–31). The Cretan leaders receive the same criticism a little later (*Politics* 1272ᵃ36–9): 'their arbitrary power of acting on their own judgement and dispensing with written law is dangerous'.

Why, then, did the Greeks begin to write down laws? If we may believe the tradition, the earliest lawgivers, Zaleukos and Charondas, were active in the seventh century BC, Zaleukos perhaps as early as the middle of the century (Zaleukos' laws are traditionally dated to 662 BC); Drakon wrote down laws at Athens in the second half of the century. The earliest stone record of a law found so far is the law from Dreros on Crete limiting tenure of the main

¹ I would like to thank Sally Humphreys, Robin Osborne, Trevor Saunders, and the editors of this volume, who all read and improved an earlier draft of this paper.

office, of perhaps 650–600 (Meiggs and Lewis 1988: no. 2). By Solon's time the custom of written law was well established, though single laws may have been more common than full-scale codification. But can we read back to this early period the aims and implications of written law visible in classical Athens? On a more general level, is written law obviously and inherently more just than a legal system which does not rely on written law? Or what is it about written law that checks—or is thought to check—arbitrary judgement and inequality of treatment? I find it hard to believe that seventh century Dreros was particularly enlightened, despite its fine inscribed law, let alone that all or even most of its citizens could read the inscription. And while Crete is famous for its extensive inscribed laws, it was precisely Cretan officials that Aristotle criticized for their use of arbitrary judgement.

Various explanations for the origin of Greek written law have been advanced: perhaps most commonly, that it was the result of popular pressure in which the people demanded that customary law be stabilized and freed from arbitrary interpretation by the aristocracy (Bonner and Smith 1930: 67, in mistaken analogy with Rome). Or that it had more conservative aims: it has recently been argued that written law in both archaic Greece and Rome was an aristocratic attempt to freeze the current legal and political conditions before revolutionary demands could erode any more of the traditional way of life (Eder 1986; Humphreys 1988: n. 9; Camassa 1988). Or that the laws were simply written down to fix them because memory and oral tradition were weakening: but once they were written down, a literate mentality developed which by its very existence enabled people to *perceive* inequality. Thus instead of written law being the product of popular demand for equality, it helped create it (C. Thomas 1977: 455–8). More puzzlingly, Gagarin's recent book sees the writing down of laws as corresponding to a 'clear and obvious need' (Gagarin 1986: 62, partly against the idea of Eastern influence). Since these laws were publicly inscribed, he argues that the first written laws reflect the development of the *polis* and its increasing interference in the lives of its citizens: 'The decision to write down a set of laws was in effect a decision to enact legislation.'[2] (But since he thinks law must by definition be written law, this is surely a circular argument.) He

---

[2] Gagarin (1986: 136). This perhaps causes him difficulties when determining the relation of procedural to substantive law: see Ruschenbusch's review (1989).

implies (p.78) that written law demonstrated the power of the *polis* and gave it more control over penalties.

Yet there is little reason to think that written law is in itself inherently democratic or egalitarian—or even simply a check on arbitrary judgement. Totalitarian regimes have been just as prone to extensive codification as democracies. And even if the laws are themselves just, the judicial machinery and political administration must correspond in order to transfer the equality of the laws to the society. Written law still needs interpretation. As Finley (1983: 30) has pointed out succinctly:'the application and efficacy of all law codes depend on the interpretation by magistrates and courts, and unless the right of interpretation is "democratized", the mere existence of written laws changes little.' In his indirect and rhetorical way, Demosthenes (21. 223-4) seems to have been aware of this when he proclaimed that the force of the laws—which were merely written letters—were made authoritative only through the *demos.*

Even in classical Athens, there was no automatic machinery to ensure that the written laws were adhered to—at least till the establishment of the *nomothetai* in 403, who in fact controlled *new* laws. Much was left to the individual knowledge of Athenian citizens: evidence that individuals did go and look at the laws is surprisingly rare, and laws could be ignored partly because no one knew of them. At the same time the 'unwritten laws'—the laws of the gods, unquestioned rules that, for example, one should look after one's parents—commanded the highest respect in the fifth century BC So even in the Athenian democracy, attitudes to written law were ambivalent and the relation of written law to the 'unwritten laws' curiously enigmatic. After 403 BC, the use of 'unwritten laws' was banned for Athenian magistrates, yet there seems to have been no statute specifically banning incest, which obviously remained prohibited by the force of social disapproval. Aristotle (*Politics* 1287b) could still say that 'customary laws (*hoi kata ta ethe*) have more weight and relate to more important matters that written law, and a man may be a safer ruler than the written law, but not safer than customary law'.[3]

The Near Eastern law codes may offer a salutary counterbalance. On closer examination, they appear even further from legal codes

---

[3] Elsewhere Aristotle stresses that even once laws have been written down, they should not always remain unaltered, *Politics* 1269ᵃ8-12; cf. 1286ᵃ9-20 on those who argue against a government acting according to written laws.

in the modern sense than we might expect. For example, the actual
function(s) of Hammurabi's Code are controversial: perhaps it represented an ideal of judgements, or it intended primarily to rein-
force the image of Hammurabi as promoting justice, rather than to
promulgate an established series of rules which everyone must
adhere to. What is clear is that the 'code' is not cited by judges in
court as one might expect of a document intended to create an
authoritative code of law; and the very form of pronouncement,
with cases often being given in the past tense, is also puzzling. It is
hard to avoid the impression that the code in its written form was
serving some kind of political or religious function (Bottéro 1982;
Finkelstein 1961; see also for Hittite law codes, Korošec 1957: 93
ff.).

In other words the mere fact that laws or legal pronouncements
have been written down is hardly enough to determine their
significance and role. We can go further: the role and implications
of writing—and therefore of written law—seem to be closely related
to the society that is using it, and not simply to some inherent qualities of the written word (Street 1984; R. Thomas 1989: ch. 1). It
is surely anachronistic to attribute characteristics of written law—
or written codification—which we take for granted now to much
earlier periods. The effect of writing in any society can vary
immensely and is partly determined by previous customs, and by
any earlier system onto which the writing is being grafted. These
previous customs must include extensive oral communication, perhaps even oral law. We therefore cannot understand the full
significance of early written law in Greece without grasping the
oral background: for example the extent of oral communication, of
customary or oral law, and the role of those early officials called
*mnemones* and therefore of sheer memory in legal procedures.
When writing was first used to record a law, it was used against
this background and must have been influenced by it. The meaning of these early written laws must also be determined by other
elements than the mere fact that they were written (and public):
for example, the character of the judges and other officials, the
mechanisms by which the law was translated into the practical giving of justice, the relation of the written law to oral and customary
law. In closer connection with the written aspect, we also need to
know who could check the written law, whether enough people
could read to ensure it was kept, the role of scribes, and perhaps

most important, the contemporary attitude to writing. It must have been this view of the use of writing, whether magical, functional, or communicative, which lay behind the attempt to write up the laws in the first place, and behind their significance once they had been written up.

We stray here into highly treacherous areas where the evidence is sparse or partial and invariably slanted in favour of what was written in stone. But they are worth exploring, partly because much that is written about Greek law (especially its early forms) seems to be influenced by ideas about written law and documents more appropriate to the modern world.[4] Most emphasis is in fact usually laid on the act itself of writing down laws, as if, once written, the laws would immediately gain a certain and obvious character.

Secondly, some recently published inscriptions concerning scribes and written laws are beginning to suggest a different slant to the role of writing and written law in Greece. Yet still the picture is confused. An excellent collection of papers on writing edited by Detienne (1988*a*) includes stimulating but directly opposed pictures of the place of written law in Greece from much the same evidence. Detienne (1988*b*) for instance, stresses the essentially public nature of Greek documents and how Greek written law made for justice, equality, and democracy (as opposed to the secret and tyrannical use of writing). Yet later in the volume Camassa (1988) tentatively discusses aspects of the social and political context which make this view hard to maintain without considerable modification, and Ruzé (1988) can point to the immense power of scribes in archaic Greece and stresses the power of writing, which should undermine any reassuring picture of openness and public written law accessible to all citizens. We seem to be left with a stark choice: was writing in early Greece a source of power or a source of openness? These two different views surely correspond to opposing views about the nature of writing. Clearly the role of those first written laws, as of writing itself, must be more complex than is usually thought.

To give this subject its due would involve much of archaic and the use of writing during that period, as well as the background of

---

[4] e.g. the idea that law is by definition written law, as in Gagarin (1986), or cf. Goody (1986: ch. 4), on how writing has affected our concept of law; Stratton (1980) is over-impressionistic.

oral communication. I concentrate here on a few aspects which must lie behind the first public use of writing and therefore the role of early written law: oral law in Section 2, unwritten law in Section 3, *mnemones* and scribes in Section 4; then I return in Section 5 to written law itself. I try to avoid archaic Athens as much as possible, since Athens and Solon tend to dominate discussion and may be rather exceptional. I will be using epigraphic evidence down to the mid-fifth century BC. It may be that my suggestions here are based on equally unusual regions, but I hope they will at least pose the possibility of a considerable variety and complexity in the development of Greek written law.

## 2. ORAL LAW

Did Greece have such a thing as oral law, that is, a body of rules that were not written down? It is sometimes held that, by definition, law cannot be oral, for only writing would be able to set law apart from other customs (Gagarin 1986);[5] or that the effect of writing down customs is to dissociate laws from custom, making law in effect primarily written law (Goody 1986: 135 ff., 144). Gagarin and others have recently insisted that the Greeks did not have oral laws as such. Yet the word *nomos* did not refer only to written law in Athens until after 403. Greek writers were quite happy with the concept of oral or unwritten laws, and we should take the implications of this seriously.

There is a surprising amount of evidence for early laws being sung (Camassa 1988: 144 f.; Weiss 1923; Piccirilli 1981; Mühl 1929; Cerri 1979). Sung laws are obviously set apart through poetry, therefore *can* be registered as a separate body of rules.[6] They also solve the problem of transmission and preservation without writing; or if they present laws which were also written down, they solve the problem of transmission amongst a population which might be illiterate.

Thus the laws (*nomoi*) of one of the earliest lawgivers, Charondas, were said to have been sung by the Athenians when

---

[5] Gagarin (1986: 10, 131) accordingly underplays the existence of 'oral laws' (though he notes the 'lawspeaker' in Iceland ).

[6] This would deal with the objection that without writing you cannot have an authoritative and definable body of rules.

drinking.[7] He enforced the singing of his laws at festivals just after the paeans 'so that the ordinances should become ingrained',[8] and according to Strabo (12. 2. 9), the Mazakenoi in Cappadocia still used his laws and had a *nomodos*, (νομῳδός) or 'law-chanter'. The use of music for educating citizens in the laws crops up in Crete, where, according to Aelian (*Varia Historia* 2. 29; cf. Strabo 10. 19c. 482), free Cretan children had to sing the *nomoi*. Terpander is said to have sung the laws of Sparta,[9] and some thought Solon tried to put his laws into verse (Plutarch, *Life of Solon* 3). In a piece of folk etymology, pseudo-Aristotle thought sung *nomoi* (i.e. 'nomes', a kind of melody) were so called 'because before men knew the art of writing they used to sing their laws in order not to forget them, as they are still accustomed to do among the Agathyrsoi' (*Problemata* 19. 28, 919ᵇ-920ᵃ). In contrast to these late and motley sources, no less sober an authority that Cicero seems to have sung the laws in his youth: he blandly recalls that, unlike nowadays, they used to learn the Twelve Tables as boys, as a 'compulsory song', a *carmen necessarium*.[10]

So the existence of sung or chanted laws was accepted without a qualm by later ancient writers. The educational value of music and poetry was taken for granted in archaic and classical Greece. Plato particularly favoured the way music infiltrated the soul (e.g. *Laws* 659ᵉ1-2, 669ᵇ5-670ᵇ6; 802ᵃ5-ᵈ6). Archaic poets were the educators and thinkers of society. Against this background of music and poetry, nothing could be more natural that the oral transmission—and performance—of laws.

The implications for written law are intriguing: if Charondas made elaborate preparations for having his laws sung as well as writing them down, then he was clearly not relying on the written text alone for transmission or even preservation. Oral transmission continued to be fundamental even once laws were written down. So there was probably no sudden change in behaviour when laws

---

[7] Hermippus fr. 88 Wehrli = Athenaios, *Deipnosophistai* 619b. Against the emendation of 'Athenians' to 'Catanians', see Piccirilli 1981.

[8] ἵν' ἐμφυσιῶται ἑκάστῳ τὰ παραγγέλματα, Stobaeus 4. 2. 24 (Hense 1911-12: 154-5).

[9] According to Clement of Alexandria, *Stromata* 1.78(Syllburg 1688: 133. 14).

[10] Cicero, *De Legibus* 2. 23, 59; cf. ibid. 2. 4. 9, which also discusses the status of written law. Cf. Martianus Capella 9. 926 (5th century AD): 'Graecarum quippe urbium multae ad lyram leges decretaque publice recitabant', 'many of the Greek cities used to recite laws and public decrees to the lyre'.

were written down (and illiteracy did not always matter). But sung laws would also help stabilize and preserve a coherent body of customary law. Could they help us recreate the atmosphere *before* the laws were written down? In other words, there is a distinct possibility that some of the earliest lawgivers fixed, or worked from, a corpus of laws which had already been transmitted orally.[11]

### 3. UNWRITTEN LAWS

There is also a wealth of evidence for the concept of 'unwritten law' (*agraphos nomos*). One would think this too showed (*a*) the existence of oral laws which were regarded as 'laws' in every important sense, and (*b*) that the Greeks were content with the concept of unwritten law. Both points have been challenged on the grounds (among others) that the term only appears in the late fifth century BC (e.g. Gagarin 1986: 25 and n. 21). Ostwald makes an elaborate analysis of all occurrences from the *Antigone* onwards, to find that each reference refers to something slightly different, thus that there was no (unified and coherent) concept of unwritten law (Ostwald 1973, against Hirzel 1900). But the evidence shows a great deal more than this. When we find that the first references to unwritten law occur in the *Antigone* performed *c*.442 (*agrapta nomima*, *Antigone* 454 f.), in the Periclean funeral speech of Thucydides (Thucydides 2. 37), and in Aristophanes' *Acharnians* of 425 (*Acharnians* 532), it is worth wondering if they do not simply reflect contemporary consciousness and debate about *written* law—and debate specifically related to the political development of Athens rather than of Greece as a whole.

You do not distinguish unwritten laws from written until you are beginning to see written law as a definite category. The fact that 'unwritten law' only begins to appear in our sources in the second half of the fifth century BC presupposes the development of a concept of *written* law, perhaps about the same time. Ostwald (1969) tried to argue that the use of *nomos* to mean specifically written law or statute began with Kleisthenes and the Kleisthenic democracy (Solon's laws were *thesmoi* not *nomoi*). But the first attested use of

[11] Though much depends on what the oral laws were about. Camassa (1988: 141–3) thus argues that there *has* to be a corpus of orally transmitted norms/'laws' before the fixation of a written code, and hints that this was so in Crete, where Eastern craftsmen may have had some influence (cf. Boardman 1980: 56–62, and Boardman 1970: 18–23).

*nomos* to denote what is apparently written law is in Aeschylus' *Suppliants* (387–91) (not absolutely certain, in fact) and *Prometheus Bound* (149 f., 402 f.), the *Suppliants* belonging to the 460s, the *Prometheus* rather later. As Ostwald (1969: 47) also admits, Euripides is the first tragedian to refer to written *nomoi* specifically and to see them as a protection against injustice (*Suppliants* 433). The term *nomos* continues to be used sometimes of unwritten law, and is the standard word for 'custom' throughout the fifth century. Mostly no distinction is made in the sources between written and unwritten rules: again, as Ostwald admits, even in the mid-fifth century BC, '*nomos* might or might not refer to written legislation; in other words, the question of writing is immaterial to the definition of a political *nomos*.'[12] What was important was that it was regarded as binding. *Nomos* does not primarily denote written law till the very end of the fifth century BC, and as Sally Humphreys (1988: 473) has pointed out, the first certain use of *nomos* as written law on an Athenian inscription is as late as 418/17 (*IG* I³ 84).[13] Not only is the use of *nomos* to mean written law rather late in the history of Greek law, but it is also extremely blurred.[14]

Nor should we neglect the background of intellectual debate. The sophists and those influenced by them in the late fifth century BC were much preoccupied with the many connotations of *nomos*: from law to custom, from merely human laws to divine ones, from custom to 'mere' convention. It looks as if the distinction between written and unwritten *nomoi* is in fact largely a product of this late-fifth-century Athenian and sophistic debate (Guthrie 1971: 117–31; rather differently, Humphreys 1988: 473 f.; cf. Ostwald 1986: 250–73). The most famous example occurs in Sophocles' *Antigone* (especially 450 ff.), where there is conflict between the laws of the state (i.e. Kreon) and the unwritten laws of the gods—here the right of burial—which have higher moral value.[15]

The discussion may well have been influenced, indeed focused, by the ability of the Athenian *demos* (citizen body) to make law

---

[12] Ostwald (1969: 44), cited aptly by Andersen (1989: 84).

[13] Though Humphreys (1987) argues that *nomos* in the 5th century BC refers rather to something old and accepted as opposed to new.

[14] Cf. the blurredness of Plato's discussions: Ostwald (1973: 95 ff.)

[15] Sophocles has been seen as a champion of unwritten law, unlike Euripides: Hirzel (1900: 69–71); but cf. Guthrie's judicious discussion (1971: 127–8).

under the radical democracy.[16] It is at this time that we first find
*written* law expressly linked with justice, in Euripides' *Suppliants*
and Gorgias' *Palamedes* (fr. 11a, § 30: written *nomoi* are the
guardians of the just). Xenophon records a conversation between
Pericles and Alcibiades about the nature of law in which Pericles
defines law as what is written down by the people—and then, with
prompting from Alcibiades, he includes even what is written down
by oligarchs, as long as the citizens are persuaded, not forced, to
accept these rules (*Memorabilia*, 1. 2. 40–6). Further on in the
*Memorabilia* the sophist Hippias questions whether justice can be
simply equated with keeping the law, since the same men can reject
or alter the very laws they have just made, whereas the unwritten
laws are the divine ones which are kept everywhere, such as the
law that you should look after your parents (*Memorabilia* 4. 4. 13
ff.; cf. also Plato, *Hippias Maior* 284d–e). Hippias' image of written
law hints at the criticisms made of the radical democracy and the
*demos*'s tendency to change its mind.

We can probably go further and associate the manipulation of
'unwritten laws' with the late-fifth-century oligarchs (some of
whom were sophists anyway): the very vagueness of the concept
made them all the easier to exploit. Some of the more disreputable
arguments of certain sophists about the promptings of nature
(which were unwritten laws too) further discredited them.[17] Plato,
hardly a democrat, comes up with some of the same ideas about
controlling the citizenry through education, custom, and 'unwritten laws' rather than written laws, as were attributed to the mythical Spartan lawgiver Lykourgos (*Laws* 793ª9–ᵈ5). Sparta prided
herself on not *needing* written laws (Plutarch, *Life of Lykourgos* 13.
3.; this is an image of Sparta more appropriate to the classical
period than earlier, since the Spartan *rhetra* was clearly a written
law: perhaps the later ideal was developed in reaction to the
Athenian democracy). The decrees of the Athenian assembly, on
the other hand, were written, and usually published on stone
(decrees/*psephismata* and *nomoi* were not formally distinguished till
after the revision of laws in 410–399 (Hansen 1978); and not

---

[16] Cf. Humphreys (1988: 473–6), noting also an implicit contrast between making law and applying it.
[17] Cf. Guthrie (1971: 22 f., 117–131). As Sealey (1984: 83) points out, a sinister remark was also attributed to Pericles, that in cases of impiety not only should
the written laws be enforced, but the unwritten ones (Lysias 6. 10).

altogether consistently then (Humphreys 1987)). Fifth-century decrees were inscribed 'so that anyone who wants can see'. This association of written publication with the *demos's* laws, an Athenian peculiarity, probably helped still more to set the 'unwritten laws' in a sinister light.

Finally, when democracy was restored in 403, it was expressly enacted that magistrates should not apply an unwritten law (Andokides 1. 85, 87), clearly a measure against the oligarchs' unscrupulous use of unwritten law, and the final binding declaration that the democracy was run on written law only.[18] This sanctified the close identification of written law with democracy, which, despite Solon's laws, seems largely a product of the climate of politics and discussion at Athens and the democratic ideal of publicity in the second half of the fifth century BC.

We can be reasonably certain, then, that in the archaic period what *we* call law and custom were barely distinguished from each other as concepts. What is distinguished in archaic and early classical inscriptions is 'what is laid down', *ho thesmos* (as Solon refers to his laws), or 'what is announced', the *rhetra* and very often simply 'the writing' (*ta grammata*), to distinguish what is written down from other norms and rules. The idea of law as a body of written rules seems to have developed in close conjunction with the political and legal experiences of fifth-century Athens.

### 4. MNEMONES AND SCRIBES

The officials variously called *mnemones* and *hieromnemones* must form a linchpin in the transition to written law. Here we can observe both the continuation of 'memory' even after writing has been introduced to record certain laws, and the importance of personnel for the role of written law when it comes. We begin to hear of *mnemones* or 'remembrancers', of course, only in inscriptions, therefore once the Greek cities have begun to record public business in writing. But the very name suggests that these officials were at

---

[18] Ostwald's attempt (1973: 91) to argue this away on the grounds that 'unwritten law' now only meant laws which were inscribed after the revision of the laws (as Andokides tries to argue) is surely over-legalistic, given the lively use of the term 'unwritten law' before this, and indeed after. Andokides is trying to argue, for his own purposes, that the law precludes those not recently inscribed, but the law as he cites it simply prohibits the *agraphos nomos*. Cf. Humphreys's rather different interpretation (1988: 476 f.), that codification was a conservative reaction.

first responsible for 'remembering'—perhaps remembering judicial cases, a living archive (as Busolt 1920 put it), sacred or secular rules, perhaps 'oral law'.[19] By definition we are unlikely to find evidence for them until public inscriptions begin in the seventh century BC. Thus the earliest attested example is the *hieromnemon* in the late-seventh-century inscription from Tiryns recording some kind of sacred law (*SEG* 30. 380, 34. 296). *Hieromnemones* occur later at fifth-century Argos (*c*.475–425 BC: Mitsos 1983: 243–9; *SEG* 33. 275), Mycenae, Crete, and Delphi. *Mnemones* occur in the Peloponnese (Nemea: twice in inscriptions, *c*.330–300 BC, *SEG* 34. 282. 11 and 34. 283), at Halikarnassos in the fifth century BC (Meiggs and Lewis 1988: no. 32), and in Crete, especially at Gortyn. Knidos has a council of *anamnamones*, and the *aisimnatai* of Megara and East Greece may have had the same function (Jeffery 1990: 20 f.; see also Busolt 1920: 362, 372 ff., 488 f.).

What do these *mnemones* do once writing spreads to their communities and is used for public record? Many of them end up as scribes—at least in Hellenistic inscriptions.[20] But do they simply become scribes and guardians of the written word? Far from it. Our evidence, scanty though it is, indicates (*a*) that they were often important officials down to the classical period, and (*b*) that they often combine their previous role as 'memorizers' with the new one of writing. Thus this is another example where writing does not take over public record completely, and where there is a more complex overlapping of memory and written record than is usually admitted.[21]

Thus the *hieromnemon* of seventh-century Tiryns is doing more than merely remembering. Whatever else is unclear in this obscure inscription, he is definitely able to impose fines (on the *platiwoinoi*, whoever they are). The *mnamon* (the Doric form of the word, used in Crete) in the fifth-century Gortyn Code is most interesting. He appears once alongside the judge as possible witness for a case

---

[19] Simondon (1982: appendix); Jeffery and Morpurgo-Davies (1970: 150); Edwards and Edwards (1977: 139); Willetts (1972: 97); Lambrinudakis and Wörrle (1983: 333 f.); cf. Kiessling (1932); Busolt (1920: 488 f., 550).

[20] See Lambrinudakis and Wörrle (1983: 328–44) for the most detailed discussion of *mnemones* for the Hellenistic period.

[21] Simondon (1982) takes memory as merely a relic of the *mnemones*' archaic function, which envisages too strict a division between memory and written record. Camassa (1988) is almost alone in noting the gradual nature of the transition to written law; the sceptical remarks of Andersen (1989: 83–4) are also relevant.

which has already been judged (Willetts 1967: col. IX .31 ff.); and an adopted son, whose (adoptive) father is renouncing the adoption, is to receive money from the father through the court and the *mnamon* (col. XI. 10 ff.; cf. also col. XI 53, and *IC* IV 42 B where the *mnamon* and judge swear an oath, and Thür, in this volume,. Later inscriptions also mention *mnamones* (*IC* IV 231, 261). The *mnamon* is closely attached to the judicial processes and to the judge himself, and if he and the judge are witnesses for the result of a past case, this hints that part of his role was to remember court proceedings (there are clearly no written court records: in another place the judge alone has to decide on oath how long it was since an order had been issued, col. I 38).[22] Neither example suggests that the *mnamon* was a simple clerk, and while he did have secretarial duties by the fifth century BC, he clearly did much more.[23] In fact, though fifth-century Gortyn was by now well accustomed to fine and extensive inscriptions of laws, the *mnamon* still remembers, the judge and *mnamon* act as witnesses for past cases. We must also compare the *mnemones* who appear on an inscription from Halikarnassos from the first half of the fifth century BC: as the inscription states, 'what the *mnemones* know is to be binding' (Meiggs and Lewis 1988: no. 32. 20-1). The powerful position of the *mnemon* could not be more explicit.[24]

These observations are crystallized in the person of Spensithios, the scribe from a community in Crete, *c.*500 BC, whose honours have been discovered inscribed, for some reason, on a bronze *mitra* or abdominal guard (Jeffery and Morpurgo-Davies 1970; also Edwards and Edwards 1974, 1977; *SEG* 27. 631). Spensithios is to be scribe or '*poinikastas*' to the city, and the office is to be hereditary. Much ink has been spilt on the word *poinikastas* and its relation to the Phoenician origin of the alphabet (but since *ta phoinikeia*

---

[22] Thus as Willetts (1967) comments (comm. *ad loc.*) on col.IX 32: 'he recorded in his memory facts relevant to the conduct of cases before the practice of writing had become widespread, esp. as here (we may presume), when cases occurred of more than usual difficulty'; or simply for any cases needing authoritative information.

[23] Ruzé (1988: 84-5) is puzzled, unnecessarily, that the secretary should be so ordinary at Gortyn while he was a novelty in Spensithios' community. No other word occurs in the Gortynian inscriptions to denote a secretary until Roman times, when *grammateus* appears, *IC* IV 257.

[24] See further, Lambrinudakis and Wörrle (1983: 333 ff.) on the early *mnemon* and his 'knowledge'. Simondon (1982: 301) takes this inscription from Halikarnassos as a quite exceptional survival of the *mnemon*'s original function.

means 'writing' anyway, there is little problem here).[25] Less attention has gone to the radical implications of the inscription for the
place of writing and scribes in the Greek city.[26]

First, his functions. His duties as 'recorder' are spelt out thus
(lines 3-5, A): ὥς κα πόλι τὰ δαμόσια τά τε θιήια καὶ τἀνθρώπινα
ποινικάζεν τε καὶ μναμονεύϝην (and this is repeated in the next
clause). Poinikazein means 'to write', mnamoneuwen recalls the office
of mnamon common in Crete and elsewhere and is usually interpreted as meaning 'to remember'.[27] So he is 'to write down and
remember the affairs of the city, both secular and divine': he seems
to be in control of all past records of the city, written and unwritten, secular and divine.[28]

But why both writing and remembering? The initial editors and
others suggest that the 'remembering' is his old function, which is
now being superseded by the use of writing, and this is his new
function.[29] But is it really being superseded? Surely he now continues to do both. The overlap, rather than merging, of written
record and memory in one individual could hardly be clearer (cf.
R. Thomas 1989: sect. 1.2.2 for examples from Athens). I would
guess this overlap occurred elsewhere in Greece. When these communities began to use writing in the public sphere, the name
mnemon was retained, memory continued to be important, and
writing did not take over public business completely. As we saw in

[25] Almost unique at the time, poinikastas has now been joined by [ph]oiniko-
grapheon ([φ]οινικογραφέων), SEG 31. 985 from Teos. poinika[ (ποινικα[) occurs at
Eleutherna, IC II 120 11, 3. ta phoinikeia (τὰ φοινικήια) at Meiggs and Lewis 1988:
no. 30B.37 from Teos; phoinikographos in two Hellenistic inscriptions from Mytilene,
IG XII 2. 96 and 97, of which the official in 97 is connected with a cult of Hermes.
On the translation of ta phoinikeia (τὰ φοινικήια) as 'writing', see e.g. Edwards and
Edwards (1977); Jeffery and Morpurgo-Davies (1970: 152); Jeffery (1967: 153 ff.)

[26] See, however, Ruzé (1988) and Camassa (1988); though Crete itself may have
been highly unusual in its approach to writing: see Stoddart and Whitley (1988).

[27] For the original editors of the inscription, the verb, not attested in Crete before,
may mean 'serve as mnamon'; Raubitschek (1970: 155-6) suggests the whole
phrase (poinikazen te kai mnamoneuwen) simply means 'record and recite' but cites no
linguistic parallel for mnamoneuwen meaning 'read aloud' only, merely the duty of
the Athenian scribe to read out old decrees. Cf. van Effenterre (1973), who inter-
prets it more broadly as the conservation of religious rules and prescriptions.

[28] Jeffery and Morpurgo-Davies the original editors, go rather further 1970:
150, suggesting that he was probably meant to formulate properly polis decisions
which were to have the force of law; he would then draft them on the wall of the
main precinct or wherever was usual.

[29] Jeffery and Morpurgo-Davies (1970); Willetts (1967: 74); Edwards and
Edwards (1977: 139) consider the terms to be probably near synonymous, the difference being that mnamon originally used memory alone.

the Gortyn Code, judge and *mnamon* had to supplement the very scanty amount of written record. It may well have been hoped that the *mnemon's* memory might ensure a certain consistency in the judicial process. But if officials were such that their very word (or oath) was enough, that was not going to change overnight with the use of writing—or of written law. The function of this writing was affected strongly by the previous customs of city and officials.

The same combination, so strange to our eyes, recurs on a recently published Tean inscription of *c.*480–450 (*SEG* 31. 985 D; Herrmann 1981; cf. also Lewis 1982 and 1990, Merkelbach 1982), which, characteristically for that city, carries another set of imprecations directed against certain officials (*timocheon* or *tamieuon*) who 'do not read out the writing on the stele to the best of their memory and power': μὴ 'ναλέξεεν τὰ γεγραθμένα ἐν τῆι [σ]τήληι ἐπὶ μνήμηι καὶ δυνάμει. It probably goes on to curse any-one who does not write the words up, or spoils the stone (it mentions a secretary again, [*ph*]*oinikographeon*, before it breaks off). The other Tean curses threatened the direst punishment on anyone who broke the stelae, cut out the letters, or made them invisible (Meiggs and Lewis 1988: no.30). *Analego* meaning 'to read out' is not so far attested on inscriptions (Herrmann 1981: 11), and the inscription might be envisaging reciting from memory. Either way we are faced with an element of memorizing—'reading out accord-ing to memory and power', or 'reciting'. Here there is a written text, yet the officials are working from memory: were they perhaps supposed to learn the inscription by heart anyway, or more loosely, were they simply not bothered about the text (cf. instances of such casualness in Athens, R. Thomas 1989: sect. 1.2.3)? Public inscrip-tions have not forced out a use of memory reminiscent of the *mnemones* elsewhere.

Evidence is too scanty to know how common this phenomenon was, and Teos was perhaps particularly neurotic about stating everything on the inscription. But if reciting the laws was fairly fre-quent, it mattered less if people could not read the inscriptions. However, there is also an element of fear here: the common archaic fear that the officials may transgress their duties (the Teans elabo-rately curse anyone who defaces the writing and also the official who does not read out the writing, cf. Debrunner Hall, this vol-ume). This brings us back to the Spensithios phenomenon and the power of the scribe.

The other astonishing thing about Spensithios is his power. It has long been a commonplace that Greece was unlike the Near East in avoiding 'scribal literacy': Greek scribes were not a specialized caste or a privileged group, for literacy was widespread, the written word was not jealously guarded, and—crucially—writing was used for casual, everyday purposes from the start (Goody and Watt 1968, for the classic statement; Detienne 1988b).[30] Yet Spensithios here receives a *misthos* or salary, and immunity from taxes, and he is to be present at and participate in sacred and secular affairs in all cases wherever the *kosmos* (or higher official) may be. He also makes the public sacrifices for certain cults where (perhaps) there is no individual priest, and his privileges are to be hereditary. Not only is Spensithios an exceedingly important individual but he is to father all future secretaries. How fair could written law be when so much was in the hands of a grand master scribe and his descendants?

The relatively sophisticated ideals of classical Athens seem very alien in this context. The Cretan *mnamones* down to the fifth century BC were full-scale officials, not mere clerks: emphasis on the problem of meaning tends to obscure the fact that Spensithios was an exceedingly powerful man. Fifth-century Teos did its best to ensure that the inscriptions were preserved and properly disseminated. And Erythrai, not mentioned so far, took extreme measures, probably in the fifth century BC, to prevent secretaries from serving the same magistrate twice and in various other ways to curb their power.[31] There is certainly no easy confidence in any of these cases that public inscriptions would safeguard the laws and justice (note the Elis decree, however, which protects the *grapheus*, c.475-450, Hainsworth 1972: no. 19; SEG 29. 402). Indeed they have recently been analysed by Ruzé (1988) to show that the Greek cities in the early stages of the public use of writing were acutely aware of the power of writing, the power of the scribe, and the power of anyone who had control of the records.[32] One must probably accept this, at least in some cases. Archaic secretaries, including those at Athens, were magistrates or officials rather than clerks.

---

[30] The idea of the Near Eastern 'scribal caste' may, however, be exaggerated: see Charpin (1986).

[31] Engelmann and Merkelbach (1972: i, 2, 17), with Ruzé (1988: 89-91). It is unclear how far this was simply a function of the secretaries being officials.

[32] Detienne (1988b: 64 ff.) also stresses their extreme importance—but that might undermine the democratic and public nature of Greek law. Note the high status of secretaries at Athens, in the 6th century BC W.V. Harris (1989: 50).

It is common elsewhere to find scribes with much wider functions than writing, for example in the Old Testament, or the English 'Recorder'.[33] Perhaps Spensithios was given such honour because scribes were fairly rare. But if they were like other officials, their power then had to be controlled. If officials are forced, on pain of being cursed, to read out the inscription, it also looks unlikely that the *demos* were expected to be able to read it themselves (lurking amongst these inscriptions are hints that only the officials could read anyway). But it is surely not just a matter of who can read. The *mnemones* in their early form as 'remembrancers' were extremely powerful too, like the Halikarnassian *mnemones* whose very 'knowledge' is to be binding (Meiggs and Lewis 1988: no. 32). So this control over the community's past records (written and unwritten) was passed on when writing began to be used by the *polis*, not created from scratch from writing alone. The effect of written record was partly, if not entirely, a function of the kind of officials who used it.

The roles of *mnemones* and scribes would suggest, then: (1) that writing was not regarded as an unmixed blessing, since scribes were often controlled; (2) that public inscriptions were not regarded as adequate guardians of the laws by themselves; and (3) that there was no sudden and simple change-over to writing. Memory continued to back up writing, literate *mnemones* continued many functions unconnected with writing. Writing, and therefore written law, did not take over completely.

## 5. THE WRITTEN LAWS

Are we any closer to understanding the significance of these early written laws or the intentions behind them? Here at least are some suggestions.

First, let us consider what actually gets written down. To judge from our evidence, very seldom is anything approaching a written code produced. The lawgivers are credited with something close to codifying activities ('writing down the laws', as if complete). But

---

[33] See Edwards and Edwards (1977: 136-8) for importance of the scribe as wider official, and his frequent connection with lawcourts. For the recorder: ibid. 136-7), but, as Andrew Lewis has pointed out to me, these developed from municipal clerks who acquired legal business because they were the only members of the corporation with legal training.

the epigraphic evidence suggests a much more gradual process, and
the extent of wholesale codification, whatever that means in a system of customary law, has probably been much exaggerated, in
optimistic analogy with Solon's law-giving. At Gortyn there was a
long succession of individual laws, and even the 'Great Code' is far
from complete (cf. Davies, this volume). At Dreros, we find individual laws written in stone at various times. We can probably assume
that the seventh century law about *kosmoi* was the only written
law of Dreros at the time. Drakon of Athens probably did not produce a lengthy 'code': his homicide law as preserved by later
Athenians may even have been an isolated pronouncement, if its
opening clause really reads (as Gagarin 1981 argued) 'even if a
man kills someone unwillingly, he is to go into exile'. It was therefore supplementing unwritten law—and presupposing its existence—rather than supplanting it.

Similarly, the evidence of the inscriptions does not fit at all well
with the literary evidence about the lawgivers. On the inscriptions
themselves, procedural law is dominant: it looks as if what gets
written on stone is not usually substantive law but procedural (as
Gagarin 1986 shows, but see n. 2 above; cf. Debrunner Hall, this
volume). That is, it must be assuming the background of substantive law—what should and should not be done—and is primarily
adding procedure, fines, and penalties. Therefore oral law is in
effect continuing long after the first laws are written up in stone:
written law does not spell the end of oral law. There is no mass
writing down of customary law (though one can see how the later
traditions came to attribute all to a single lawgiver). This also suggests that writing, or at least public writing on stone, was
specifically and deliberately used for the judicial side of the *polis*, for
controlling procedure and magistrates, but not for the values and
beliefs that could be easily held orally. This is visible even in Sparta.
The 'Lykourgan laws' which supposedly governed the peculiarly
Spartan way of life were the unwritten customs enforced by her
educational system; the great Spartan *rhetra*, which somehow got
written down, was a law about procedure, albeit important constitutional procedure.

So written law on stone was perhaps intended to fix the kind of
law or pronouncement which was not universally recognized.[34]

[34] It is unclear, however, how easy it would be to discern change in customary
law, if that was even an object: was it actually *believed* to be unchanging (as

There could hardly be a more efficient way of preserving and fixing an enactment than setting it in stone. The Gortyn 'Code' refers obsessively to 'the writing': judges are to judge 'according to the writing' or they must 'decide on oath' (references to 'what is written' occur at least twenty-four times in the Great Code, Ruzé 1988: 85 n. 9). Stringent punishment is therefore threatened if anyone defaces the stone.[35] Even if most people could not read them, the inscriptions could at least be seen in a public place, and if officials had to read them out, their content could be widely known. (However, there was still much that was not written down at all, and it is important to ask who it is who decides to fix the law.)

But how could they have enforced procedure, or controlled magistrates, if this was their desired effect? (Most discussions seem to imply that writing up the rules was enough.) As we have seen, cities did attempt to control their officials, including the scribes, who were evidently not always trusted. But what were the real sanctions against disregarding a law? And were there any real mechanisms to deal with an offender? Solon was probably most unusual in setting up a mechanism by which any citizen could prosecute, the *graphe*, as opposed to the *dike* which was initiated primarily by the wronged person himself. But many of the earliest laws on stone seem to leave no room for such a procedure. Often the wronged person is to fall back on 'self-help'. So the law is only stating an ideal. Or, as in a Chios law (Hainsworth 1972: no.74 = Collitz 1884–1915: no. 5653), if a guilty official fails to enforce a fine, he has to pay it, and if he does not, it must be paid by the next officials up ('the fifteen'), and if they don't pay, they are to be cursed. So the law is in effect enforced by superior officials.

Remarkably often, however, the sanctions seem rather to be religious ones. The sanctions are frequently in the form of oaths: for example the seventh-century Dreros law regulating ambitious *kosmoi* ends with a list of those who are 'swearers'. It is not clear if they were swearing to obey or to enforce the law, but this oath was surely the main hope of enforcing the law (and those forced to swear would presumably be the main potential transgressors of the

Camassa 1988: 148 suggests) or was it mainly penalties which became disputed? In fact change may only become visible once law is written down.

[35] Meiggs and Lewis 1988: no.17. 7–10 (*c*.500 BC); no. 30.35–41 (Tean curses); Mitsos (1983). Cf. also the curse on the later Parian inscription, Lambrinudakis and Wörrle 1983: lines 7 ff.).

law). Or else the sanctions are in the hands of the gods. The enthu-
siastic use of curses at Teos actually represents the enlistment of
religious sanctions against secular offenders.[36] Indeed when the
officials in Teos are to 'read out the stele according to their memory and power', they are in effect to read out the curses, and the
inscription is more the record of a curse than a law. The Lokrian
law about settling new territory (Meiggs and Lewis 1988: no. 13)
begins *tethmos hode*, 'this law' (= *thesmos*), but this law is to be
sacred to 'Pythian Apollo and the gods that dwell with him': 'may
there be destruction on those who transgress it but may the god be
kind to him who observes it' (lines 14-16). Or in a couple of
treaties we find a sacred fine (ibid. no.17, *c*.500 BC), or that the
guarantors of the treaty are to include Zeus and Apollo (ibid. no.
10).

The fact that these inscriptions may state a decision of the *polis*
is often emphasized as showing the beginning of state apparatus,
the *polis's* legislative power, and the *polis's* self-awareness. What is
less often noted is how often these laws (right down to the fifth century BC) are actually under the protection of the gods. Many also
begin with an invocation to a god (Dreros, the Spensithios inscription). In other words it is not the writing in stone that is to make
these laws effective and enforceable, but the gods, the curses or
other sanctions which belong rather to the realm of what Gernet
(1976) called 'pre-law'. Detienne has stressed how often these early
inscriptions are under divine protection.[37] Yet surely that divine
protection sets the fact of their written form in an unexpected and
peculiar light. The fact that they are written law does not seem to
be enough to make the laws valid, as is so often implied. There is
a conscious effort to include non-legislative sanctions.

One wonders, then, whether the writing itself was seen in a
superstitious light? Should we perhaps say that the writing of a law
on stone helped to crystallize the religious sanctions or perpetuated
the curse in a more authoritative way? Or that writing was seen
as a way of making the law into a physical object that was more

---

[36] On public imprecations, Ziebarth (1895), who stresses the use of curses as
sanctions well beyond the classical period, and Vallois (1914), are important; also
Latte 1964: 68-77); Lambrinudakis and Wörrle (1983: 310-13); Wilhelm (1951:
86); Humphreys (1988: n. 22). Hainsworth (1972: no. 74) also mentions a 'customary' set of curses.

[37] Detienne (1988b: 51-3; see 52 n. 80 for other references). Cf. also the use of
religious sanctions in Roman law: for example, Williamson (1987: 174-8).

easily put under the protection of the god, even dedicated in its material form to the god?[38] What is clear is that early public writings (i.e. laws) are often associated with temples, written up on temple walls or set in the precinct. And one of the earliest uses of writing in Greece, attested by 650–625 BC, is for writing curses which are then left in a sanctuary (Langdon 1976: 42, Hymettos; cf. the early graffiti on an *aryballos* from Cumae of *c*.675–650 cursing whoever steals it, *IG* XIV 865; Jeffery 1990: 238, no. 3). The other common use is for dedications. Attitudes to writing are highly variable and help determine its very use. Perhaps the monumental stone inscription in the sanctuary was an attempt to give political and procedural rulings the status of the unwritten laws, heavily buttressed by divine authority.

We are, at any rate, far from the democratic Athenian ideal of written law. Not only does the epigraphic evidence suggest that laws were often written down gradually and in piecemeal fashion, but their role and intentions cannot be deduced merely from the fact that they were written. Behind these early inscribed laws lay customs and ideas which must partly have been inherited from the realm of customary and oral law and the *mnemones*; also certain attitudes to the written word which differed from those in later periods and perhaps from *polis* to *polis*. What emerges above all is the strikingly sacred context of so much of early public writing and written law.

### 6. CONCLUSIONS

Most discussions of the role of early Greek law look down the centuries from periods where written law was well established and writing paramount. I have tried to put archaic written law more firmly into its contemporary context and have approached it from the other side: this involves not simply the political background but the role of writing and the usually invisible presence of oral or customary law (which did indeed exist).

In later Greece written law was indeed held to be a check on arbitrary judgement, and in Athens was central to the democracy. The original reasons for writing down law, whatever they were, do not

---

[38] Cf. Jensen's suggestion (1980: 93–4) that when the Delians put the Homeric Hymn to Apollo (1. 320–21) on a whitened board and presented it to the goddess, this was simply to give it physical form so that it could be dedicated.

alter this. Written law can be—and often is—fundamental in checking arbitrary judgement: when justice was in the hands of a few elders and governed by unwritten law, it was clearly open to arbitrary judgement and inconsistency. The fact that so many archaic communities were determined, once they had a set of laws, that they should not change, suggests that one anxiety had been that the laws might indeed change: writing down a law on stone was meant partly to stabilize it for evermore.

But there must be more to it than that. In the archaic period written law probably represented the first encroachment of writing into the sphere of public life. Given the complexity of writing and its possible uses, it is reasonable to expect that the archaic use of writing for laws was influenced by customs and ideas already present; that writing did not change everything immediately, and that attitudes to the new medium were tinged with contemporary concerns and beliefs, not later ones. Thus, as we have seen, unwritten law often continued alongside written law, rather than being forced out by it. Officials responsible for their memory and 'knowledge' continued to be so long after the first laws were written down. Similarly the first scribes inherited their predecessors' (oral) responsibilities alongside the new duties connected with writing. Scribes were treated not as neutral repositories of records (as many modern scholars would have it) but just like other officials. Some cities were highly conscious of the scribe's power, but was this through fear of the power of writing itself, or because the scribe was seen as yet another official who, in true archaic fashion, must be closely supervised? At any rate, the role of writing was affected by the society already there. The officials concerned with written record were as powerful—and perhaps as distrusted—as their predecessors. Writing down the laws alone cannot therefore have created equality before the law.

As for the laws themselves, not only does the epigraphic evidence suggest that laws were often written down gradually and in piecemeal fashion, but their role and intentions cannot be deduced merely from the fact that they were written. Behind these early inscribed laws lay customs and ideas which must partly have been inherited from the realm of customary and oral law and the *mnemones*. Too many examples suggest that written law supplemented rather than superseded unwritten law for us to ignore the possibility that only certain kinds of law got written down in the first place. So we need to ask not only about contemporary attitudes to writing—which may also have varied from *polis* to *polis*—but also whether writing, or writing on stone specifically, was reserved for particular types of legislation, and why. What emerges so strikingly is the sacred context of so much of early public writing. (As Connor (1988) has recently emphasized, civic and political activity is permeated even in the classical period by sacred ritual and concern for the divine, which would suggest that this sacred context would be a further expression of the convergence of sacred and secular in the good running of the state.) The legislators were not relying on the written form alone to make the laws effective: these laws seem rather to be guaranteed by the gods or other religious sanctions. So why were they so elaborately written out on stone? What I have tentatively suggested is that the monumental inscription of a law was intended not only to fix it publicly in writing, but to confer divine protection and a monumental impressiveness on just those kinds of law which did not receive the time-honoured respect accorded the unwritten laws and customs. In later Athens, the inscribing of decrees on stone symbolized publicity and democratic decision-making. In earlier times the inscription added weight and divine protection. It was precisely laws about procedure and constitution which so desperately needed them.

This chapter originally appeared as an article in the *Bulletin of the Institute of Classical Studies*, 40 (1995).

# 3

# Deconstructing Gortyn: When is a Code a Code?

## JOHN K. DAVIES

### 1. INTRODUCTION: THE 'LAW CODES' OF GORTYN

Discussion of Greek law beyond Athens has tended to look first, for good reasons, at Gortyn in Crete, the only alternative source of extensive documentation in the classical period. Even so, and in spite of Margherita Guarducci's exemplary publication of the material in 1950, detailed study of it has been very thin on the ground till recently,[1] with the honourable exception of the series of studies by Ronald Willetts which culminated in his re-edition of the Great Code in 1967.[2] Some more recent work, notably by Michael Gagarin, has advanced the discussion, but it remains concentrated very largely on the Code, whether as documentary evidence of substantive law or as the reflection of social customs and values.

Such an approach leaves major questions unasked. In this paper, following a lead given by Lemosse (1957) but subsequently neglected, I shall attempt to subvert it in favour of the following propositions: (a) that the Code has to be seen as part of a corpus of documentation; and (b) that its format has to be seen within a framework of revision of law which moves both towards and away from codification.

It is convenient to begin by reviewing the evidence. No fewer than a quarter of the surviving Greek inscriptions of Crete come from Gortyn, that superficially unexceptional town at the upper (eastern) end of the Mesara plain which the experienced Roman eye

---

[1] The only relevant references (i.e. to *IC* IV 1-159) in *SEG* are: 12. 402-4; 13. 468; 15. 574-5; 16. 533; 18. 393; 19. 605-6; 23. 585-7; 24. 1162; 25. 1041-3; 27. 731, 734, 736; 29. 825; 30. 1110; 31. 811; 32. 867-8; 33. 731; 35. 982-3; 36. 810; 37. 744-5; 38. 899; 39. 960-2; 40. 772-3. There is an equally thin harvest in *Bulletin Épigraphique*.

[2] For a (hopefully complete) list see the bibliography and Bile (1988: 26-7). There are warning notes against some of Willetts's assumptions in Meyer-Laurin (1969).

for landscape picked on as the capital of the province of Crete and Cyrene. Among these inscriptions, notoriously, is the Great Code (*IC* IV 72), but it does not emerge from nowhere. Within Crete Gortyn is only one of eight cities from which fragments of early codes survive (Jeffery 1990: 310: the others are Axos, Dreros, Ellynia, Lyttos, Eleutherna, Prinias, Knossos). Within Gortyn itself the Code is only one, albeit by far the largest, of a lengthy series, grouped by Guarducci as *IC* IV 1-159, all written retrograde or boustrophedon, all dating from the archaic and classical periods, and all save one (*IC* IV 50) concerned with public law in one way or another. Even if we leave aside some eighty six of these documents (*IC* IV 18-19, 24-9, 31-40, 48-9, 54, 59-61, 66-70, 92-140, 151-9) as being such miserable scraps that the subject-matter cannot be discerned with certainty or at all, there remain seventy three substantive documents. That they vary in script, format, and find-spot shows that they were not created as a unity but are to be distributed throughout the period from the first publication of documentation on stone (early sixth century BC?) till the early or middle fourth century BC: at that time there appears to have been a clear horizon of public sensibility, marked alike epigraphically by the abandonment of boustrophedon writing, and in subject-matter, by the increasing rarity of documents which are laws rather than treaties or decrees or letters (*IC* IV 160 is transitional—though it is law it is not boustrophedon). We may with Guarducci put that horizon somewhere in the early or middle fourth century BC, and may account for it in various ways, but it is real, and requires that discourse be about a group of documents promulgated over 200-250 years. The questions which pose themselves are therefore not those generated by a single document in isolation, but must above all be those generated by a series, viz. about their interrelationship to each other and especially to *IC* IV 72; about changes in law or in social and political values; and about the nature and purpose of the sort of archivization of public action which is represented by the promulgation of documents in a public and long-lasting format.

We have only the documents themselves to guide us, and must therefore begin with them. They vary enormously in size. At one extreme is the Great Code, with its twelve columns, all but the last comprising about fifty-five lines each; at the other is the apparently complete but enigmatic *IC* IV 22B, with all of five words.[3] Clearly, however, *IC* IV 72 was not the only large-scale document planned as a unit. For our purposes there are two kinds of comparanda:

1. Archaic documents comprising (probably) a single ordinance, but spread over 15 stones (*IC* IV 8), or 13 (*IC* IV 9), 9 (*IC* IV 11), 18 (*IC* IV 12, 14), 12 (*IC* IV 13), or even, at the extreme, 44 (*IC* IV 10), which was set out as one or two lines of writing going round the four sides of the steps or the walls of a building such as the temple of Pythian Apollo. These are documents significant indeed for what they reveal of a (presumably sixth century BC) taste for the monumental, instinct for permanence, and competence in planning; but they are less relevant for us than

2 Those set out (like *IC* IV 72) in columns. Those surviving in this category are no fewer than twenty-two. Most of them, inevitably being fragmentary, present evidence only of two columns,[4] but two (*IC* IV 53 and 77) had at least three, and two others (*IC* IV 75 and 41) had four or more.

In this last group, *IC* IV 75, a document to which we shall return, presents four columns, of which A lays down procedure to deal with the case of land erroneously marked off as security for a loan; B lists goods, mostly household goods, and is interpreted in the light of Diodoros 1. 79. 5 as a list of goods which could not be seized as pledges; C provides for the procedure whereby a proxy can act in pledge proceedings; and D is wholly unclear. The positive indications are therefore that *IC* IV 75 presents systematic regulations about pledging/security, but since regulations on various aspects of pledging are found not only in two contexts of *IC* IV 72 (cols. I and VI 46 ff.) but also on ten other documents (*IC* IV 30, 41; V/VI 43A, 45, 47, 81, 85, 86, 91, 102) we most certainly cannot say that *IC* IV 75 is *the* Gortynian law about pledging and security.

The remaining complex document is *IC* IV 41, which had at least eight columns. Of those, the extreme right-hand column is hopeless; column I deals with compensations for an animal injured or

[3] *IC* IV 22B: πρόθεσιν μη̑τ' ἀ[πο]δικάζαι μη̑τ' ἀπομ[όσαι. Translation not certain. Either '(the relatives of a dead person) may not avoid his laying out, either by seeking court action or by entering an oath of denial', or '(persons) may not evade statutory time limits, either by seeking court action or by entering an oath of denial'.

[4] *IC* IV 42, 43, 45–7, 52, 54, 65, 73, 74, 76, 82, 90, 103, 107, 110, 140. *IC* IV 51 is also said to have been laid out in columns.

killed by another animal; II deals specifically with equids which are injured or killed; III may start by dealing with damage wrought by dogs, but then deals with penalties for the non-return of animals and birds which have been lent—a theme which *may* continue into IV but then there is an abrupt switch to fugitive slaves, while V and VI switch equally abruptly to *nexus* (debt bondage), V laying down the responsibility for acts committed by a person who has pledged himself, VI splitting between him and his creditor damages for hurt inflicted upon him; and VII starts off about (damaged?) goods and animals being brought to a temple, and then shifts to detailing who should compensate for damage inflicted by a slave whose ownership is changing hands.

It would just be possible to see *IC* IV 41 as a document conceived as a whole and dealing in general with responsibility for damages, but that is not the most obvious reading of it, not least because the amount of text lost at the top of each column is wholly uncertain: it is safer and wiser to see *IC* IV 41 and perhaps *IC* IV 75 too, if not others, as being documents like *IC* IV 72, i.e. assemblages of rules on various matters put together as a single utterance in virtue of some principle of unity which it is our business to try to discover.

## 2. HOW CODIFIED IS THE GREAT CODE?

What I have said so far is intended to provide a framework of reference, partly for the Gortynian legal inscriptions in general, partly for the Great Code in particular. I now turn to the latter in rather more detail. At first and second sight its format is exceptionally lucid. Topics, though not flagged by any heading such as one might find in Athens,[5] or by any indentation or fresh line-start as on some of the older boustrophedon inscriptions of Crete (Jeffery 1990: 311; Willetts 1967: 4), are clearly identifiable, as the summaries of Willetts 1967 and Gagarin 1982 reveal, while individual sections on identifiable topics are separated by asyndeton (conjunctions and other linking words are absent). Whether, as Gagarin argues (1982: 138 ff.), vacats (spaces left deliberately blank) indicate systematically thought-out subsections within a section, rather than

---

[5] e.g. the headings *pemptei* ('on the fifth day'), *hektei* ('on the sixth day'), etc. in the Great Calendar of sacrifices (Oliver and Dow 1935: 8-32, nos. 2-3, lines 3-4, 6, and 23-4), or the subheadings on the 4th-century-BC navy-lists (e.g. *IG* II² 1613, lines 60-1, or *IG* II² 1622 *passim*).

faults in the stone (as Willetts 1967: 4 believes), is perhaps more moot, but even without that it is very tidy. What is more, if admittedly we discount three intrusive topics at the turn of columns VI and VII (Willetts's items 12–14; Gagarin's items 18–20), and if we discount most of column I, which is about rules for the seizure of persons of disputed (slave/free) status, then it is possible to say with Gagarin (1982: 135):

The structure revealed by asyndeton on the one hand confirms the traditional view that the Code is not a systematic and comprehensive set of laws: on the other hand, however, it reveals a greater organization of provisions than is sometimes acknowledged. . . Thus about two-thirds of the main body of the code consists of regulations about the family and its property, and some attempt was clearly made to group together related sections.

The trouble is that this will not do: not only is the material which one has to discount in order to reach such a conclusion very substantial, but there are other even more intractable obstacles. Let me set them out systematically.

1. The first is purely formal, that columns XI 24 ff. to the end are cut in a different hand from the main body of the document (cf. Fig. 1 or the facsimiles of Guarducci (1950) or Willetts (1967) for the different lambdas and thetas). However, what the facsimiles also make clear is a point which has been insufficiently weighed in the literature. Columns I–XI all begin at the same level/course of stones: the absence of the stone which carries the top of X is pure accident, and there are extant fragments which may come from it (Willetts 1967: 4a). Column XII in contrast *seems* to start one course down—I say 'seems' because one cannot be quite certain that the original stone (stone L), rather than the replacement which now figures in photographs, was anepigraphic, but column XII makes sense as it stands, and what is more, the top left-hand corner of the stringer which starts column XII carries the letters '*IBA*' (= 12a). That is to say, it was the first stone of the column and was numbered as such when the stones were re-used in the first century BC (Willetts 1967: 4a; Keyser 1987). The problem is whether one infers from this simply that there was already something in the space occupied by stone L, such as a window (Guarducci 1950: 126) or an existing inscription, or whether one infers that XI 24 ff. and XII were inscribed *after* columns I–XI had

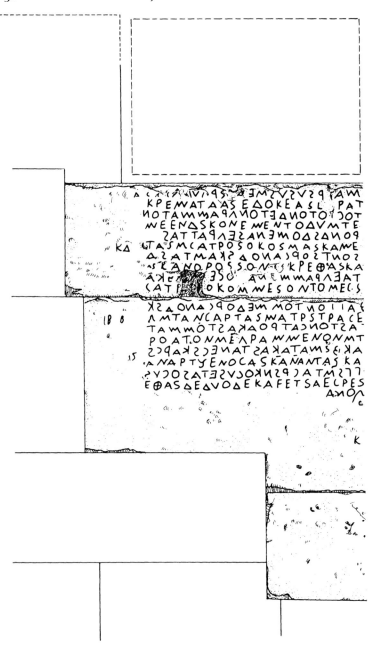

FIG. 1. *IC* IV 72 cols. X–XII

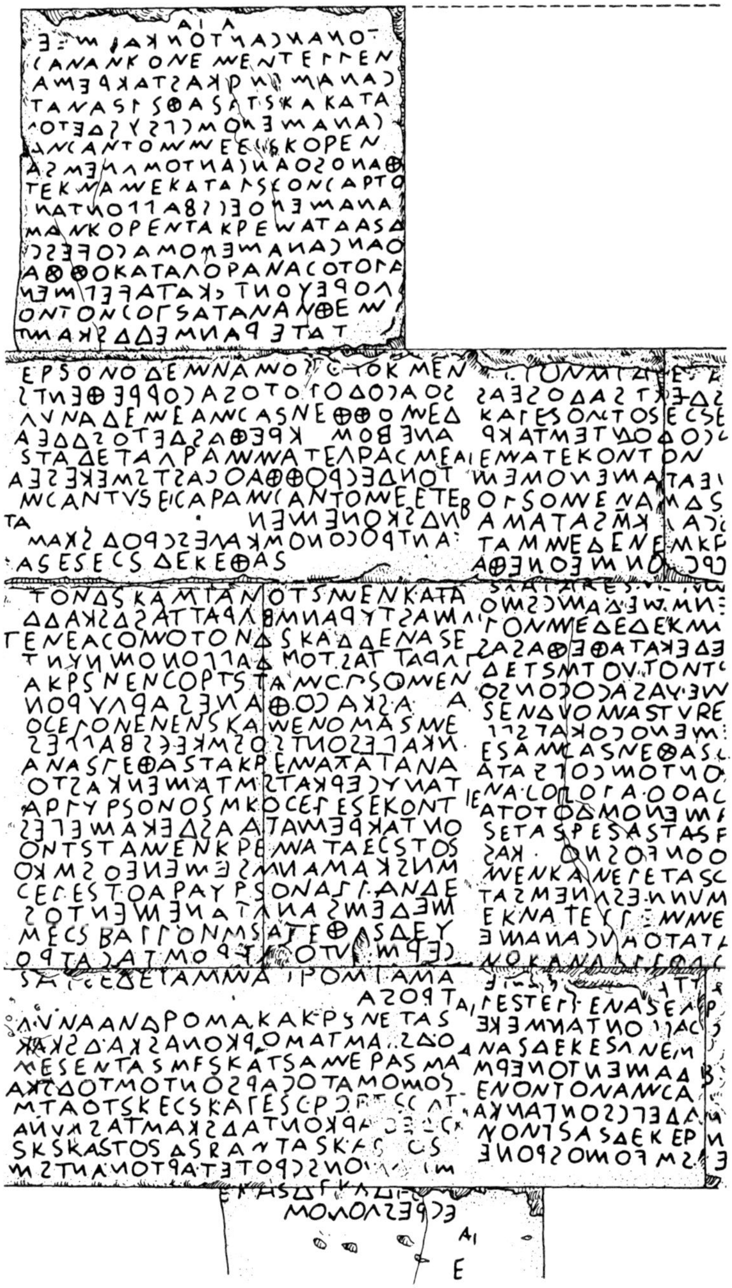

already been planned and cut as a unit. Given the content of the additional material, which largely comprises amendments to earlier sections, the latter hypothesis seems to me far more likely, thereby posing immediate questions about the processes of formulation and validation.

2. The second obstacle is that the degree of systematization is extremely variable.

(*a*) At one extreme stands the law on adoption, cols. X 33 to XI 23. This begins in a general statement (X 33-4): 'adoption is to be from wherever one wishes', the determining social importance of which I need not emphasize, and goes on to specify procedure (ll. 34-9) and the obligations incumbent upon the adoptee (ll. 39-48), a section which refers to, and incorporates, pre-existing legislation ('as is written for legitimate children', ll. 44-5, 46). Lines 48 ff. pick up the logic of lines 41-2 to lay down what happens if there *are* legitimate children of the adopter; lines 49-52 if there are males, lines 52 to XI 6 if females. Lines XI 6-10 envisage the circumstance of the adoptee himself dying childless, lines 10-17 envisage the circumstance of the adopter renouncing the adoptee, and the section ends with restrictions on the capacity to adopt (ll. 18-19) and with a clear prescription of validation of property held in terms of earlier arrangements (ll. 19-23). This really is codification: a general principle is enunciated, whether enabling or prohibitory (here enabling), a cross-reference to existing law is inserted, and the likely circumstances arising from its application are envisaged and systematically provided for—altogether a model of a modern major general law.

(*b*) In contrast, lines II 2-45 on rape, seduction, and adultery are really rather a mess. First of all, we have varying phrases for the sexual misdemeanour under discussion: κάρτει οἰπεῖ, *kartei oipei* (l. 3); κάρτει δαμάσαιτο, *kartei damasaito* (ll. 11-12); ἐπιπέρεται οἶπεν, *epiperetai oipen* (l. 17); μοικίον, *moikion* (ll. 21, 44)—but the differences between these acts are nowhere defined, even though the variations in penalties are extreme, ranging as far as the possibility of lynching (ll. 34-6) (see fig. 2). Granted, the definition of terms is something almost wholly foreign to Greek law,[6] so the degree of clarity to be expected is limited, but even so we might expect some distinction between (say) seduction and rape.

---

[6] Though the Code does actually define an heiress at one point: *IC* IV 72 col. VIII. 40-2.

| Victim | Rapist | | | Offender Seducer | Adulterer | |
|---|---|---|---|---|---|---|
| | free man | slave | male serf | free man? | free man | slave |
| free man | 100 st. (2–4) | 200 st. (5–7) | | | | |
| free woman: | | | | | | |
| in relative's house | 100 st. (2–4) | 200 st. (5–7) | | 10 st. | 100 st. (20–3) | 200 st. (26–7) |
| in another's house | | | | | 50 st. (23–4) | 100 st. (26–7) |
| *apetairos* | 10 st. (4–5) | | | | | |
| wife of *apetairos* | | | | | 10 st. (24–5) | |
| male serf | 5 dr. (7–9) | | 5 st. (9–10) | | | |
| female serf | 5 dr. (7–9) | | 5 st. (9–10) | | | |
| household slave: | | | | | | |
| virgin | 2 st. (11–16) | | | | | 5 st. (27–8) |
| already seduced by day | 1 ob. (13–15) | | | | | |
| already seduced by night | 2 ob. (13–15) | | | | | |

st. = stater; dr. = drachma; ob. = obol
6 obols = 1 drachma; 2 drachmai = 1 stater
numbers in () = line numbers

Fig. 2  Matrix of Penalties in *IC* IV 72 col. II

Secondly, and more substantially, the matrix of penalties set up by the social necessity to take account of the range of possible legal statuses of offender and victim is only very patchily filled out—not all possible combinations are included (see Fig. 2, retaining the units of measure of the text). The difficulty is to decide whether the gaps derive from unsystematic thought, from the unlikelihood or non-penalizability of the offence, or from the existence elsewhere of complementary rules. The lack of specified penalty for adultery by a free man with a slave, for example, can hardly be due to non-penalizability, since (a) lines 27-8 show slaves are envisaged as capable of being the victims, and (b) the act should presumably count as damage to another person's property anyway. Likewise serfs are not explicitly envisaged either as agents or as victims of adultery, though they are of rape: and yet, as is patent on Fig. 2, the matrix for rape is just as full of gaps as that for adultery. Thirdly, the provisions in lines 28-45 for ransoming the adulterer caught in the house are equally untidy. In lines 28-33 the only statuses envisaged for such an adulterer are free (implicitly) or slave: but in lines 36 ff., envisaging the contingency that the arrested adulterer may claim that he has been captured by subterfuge, the statuses named are *apetairos* ('not full citizen')[7] and serf (ll. 40-2), while the category described in lines 38-9 as 'a case involving 50 staters and more' does indeed cover four of the cases in the adulterer matrix but leaves the adulterer of the wife of an *apetairos* in limbo. Either all this is crass incompetence, or the authors of these laws are not setting out to be as systematic and complete as we think they are or ought to have been.

3. A third obstacle to reading the Great Code as a code, or at any rate as a successful code, comes from the content of the apparent additions and corrections to the main body of the Code in columns XI-XII. In the following section I shall survey it very briefly, but none the less in some detail for reasons which will become apparent.

3. SUPPLEMENTARY/EMENDATORY MATERIAL (COLS. XI-XII):

---

[7] For the problems involved in translating *apetairos*, see Willetts (1967: 12-13) and Laurencic (1988).

## 3. SUPPLEMENTARY/EMENDATORY MATERIAL (COLS. XI–XII): THE PROBLEMS

Lines XI 24–5, brief but fundamental, are seen by the commentators (Willetts 1967: 34. 18(*a*); Gagarin 1982:131, sect. 31 (30)) as supplementing partly I 2 ff. ('whosoever may be likely to contend about a free man or a slave [i.e. about his status] is not to seize him before trial') and partly X 25–32, which protect a pledged man, or one engaged in legal process, from being bought. Collectively it all amounts to a Habeas Corpus Act protecting men whose legal status is the subject of contention, but the lack of cross-reference, and the introduction of the new element of 'receiving in asylum' (if that is the right interpretation of *epidekesthai*), raise the question to what extent lines XI 24–5 were envisaged as supplementation rather than new laws.

Lines XI 26–31 (Willetts 1967: 34. 18(*b*); Gagarin 1982:131, sect. 31 (31)), on the two distinct functions of a judge, are again fundamental. They are new and have no correlate anywhere in the Codes.

The provisions in lines XI 31–45 (Willetts 1967: 34. 18(*c*); Gagarin 1982: 131, sect. 31 (32)), quite clearly pick up and supplement IX 24–40 on obligations owing from a dead man. The basic gist in column IX was that creditors should bring suit within the year (whether before the end of the official year or before twelve months have elapsed is not clear), with details about procedure. Column XI in contrast lays out the various choices for the heirs (accept the inheritance and pay the debt, or receive neither).

Lines XI 46–55 (Willetts 1967: 34. 18(*d*); Gagarin 1982: 131, sect. 31 (33)) are more closely connected with what has preceded. The section from II 45 to III 16 comprises a very clearly laid-out set of rules about what a wife may take away with her in case of divorce. Part of them stated (III 5 ff.): 'But as regards things which she denies (i.e. having taken away), the judge is to adjudge (*dikaksai*) that the woman take an oath of denial by Artemis.' At this point the drift of the supplement before us in column XI is obviously to clarify this element of procedure, partly by laying down a time-limit for that oath to be taken, partly by building in an interval of notice of suit and by requiring a witness of some age and standing.

The brief provision in lines XII 1–5 (Willetts 1967: 34.18(*e*); Gagarin 1982: 131, sect. 31 (34)) can be plugged in even more closely and satisfyingly. Lines X 14-20 lay down a limit of 100 staters for gifts from son to mother or husband to wife. Column XII reaffirms that, with a cross-reference, while withdrawing the possibility of suit over arrangements, even if different (i.e. larger), made before the law was passed.

Lastly under this heading, lines XII 6-19 (Willetts 1967: 34. 18(*f*); Gagarin 1982: 131, sect. 31 (35)), which adds yet more to the longest section of the Great Code, that on heiresses (really girls with no father or brothers) and their property, and does so in a thoroughly subversive way. The jumping-off point in the main Code for our purposes is lines VIII 42-53, which lay down rules for who administers the property of an heiress until she is of age to marry. Here it is stated quite lucidly that the pecking order starts with (*a*) the father's brothers, the heiress taking half the produce of the property. However, it is implicit that one of the father's brothers is likely to be the groom elect in terms of the provision at VII 15: 'the heiress is to be married to the brother of her father, the oldest of those living.' Hence the provision in VIII 47 says in effect (though not specifically) that (*b*) if there are no father's brothers, then the girl herself is in charge as beneficial owner, brought up by her mother, but that (*c*) if she has no mother, then her mother's brother inherits and becomes groom elect.

Column XII varies this in three respects:

1. It introduces officials called *orpanodikastai* ('orphan-judges'), but via the peculiarly illogical route of saying that these regulations apply if there are none in post. The new provision does not specify what is to happen if these officials *are* in post;

2. It replaces stages (*b*) and (*c*) above with a provision for joint administration by a paternal and a maternal relative (if the interpretation is right), who are *tons egrammenons* (written, registered, nominated?); and

3. It lays down a minimum age for marriage.

Even apart from the lengthy section on heiresses in the Code, there are at least two other documents which certainly or probably regulate their circumstances (*IC* IV 44, 56), though regrettably too small and fragmentary to reveal their substantive provisions. Historically, i.e. socially and politically, this was clearly an area of major friction and of change in Gortyn in the sixth and fifth centuries BC. I am not here concerned primarily to trace and explain the direction of that change (see Willetts 1967: 23 ff.), but only with the consequences for statutory provision. Specifically what we seem to have here in columns VII–IX and XII is a major piece of clarifying codification initially comparable in format and quality of thought to the section on adoption, which then has to be re-muddled in order to incorporate new ideas and new officials.

Though of course this is pure hypothesis, it looks to me as if the political process, i.e. public opinion/prejudice as represented by the assembly, has wrong-footed the lawmaking process in two ways: (a) by declining to accept the eventuality implicit in the provisions outlined in the Great Code that the administration of an heiress's estate could be taken over by her mother's family completely if there were no father's brother available, and instead insisting that the paternal family keeps a foothold somehow; and

(b) by creating, or resuscitating memory of, the officials called *orpanodikastai*, who appear nowhere else in the Code, even in contexts like lines III 44 to IV 23 on children born after divorce or born out of wedlock, where they well might, nor anywhere else in extant texts. In consequence the lawmakers have incorporated these points in an amendment while rescuing as much of the original formulation as they could.[8]

I have dwelt on columns XI–XII at some length as being procedurally the most revealing piece of the Code. I am obviously taking as true the proposition that the items in these columns are amendments or subsequent additions, and am trying to elicit from them some hint of what the processes and pressures were which led to the Great Code (i.e. the whole document which we have) presenting simultaneously the appearance of a movement towards codification and systematization and the appearance of a movement away from it. For the last section, on heiresses, I have just suggested feedback from the political arena as the source. For others, such as the quasi-jurisprudential section on the twin functions of judges, there is no basis for even guessing. For the remainder, where positive law is concerned and where it is a matter of defining a grey area or making procedures explicit, the possibility should at least be aired that we are dealing with a form of case law. It could

---

[8] I do indeed wonder whether via the words *tons egrammenons* they are referring not to a process of registering the guardians of the property (still less 'nominating', Willetts 1967: 34. 18(*f*), for which the word *egrammenons* is wholly inappropriate), but to other statutory provisions which they had hitherto disregarded, by accident or design: but my argument does not depend on that speculation.

be argued that the application of columns I–XI to actual suits had revealed gaps or loose edges here and there, which are remedied via formulations which are patchwork but which are generally applicable law, not one-off decisions.

At this point it may be appropriate to do a large Herodotean loop before returning to the Code and to questions of its promulgation and validation. If, as is generally and surely rightly assumed, behind large-scale systematizations such as we have in *IC* IV 41 and *IC* IV 72 lie older, perhaps less well thought-out or less closely interconnected sets of regulations, then the question must be whether the epigraphic records outside the Great Code allows us to see the processes of law-creation at work. Up to a point they do, if we look at overlaps, repetitions, and the general questions of format and grouping.

First, then, overlap and repetition, there being one clear example of each. The example of overlap is all the more revealing for linking a column of the earlier code (*IC* IV 41) with the later Great Code (*IC* IV 72). Both passages deal with damages or injury brought about by a slave who has changed hands by purchase, the problem being to sort out which owner should have the responsibility for making good the damages. The earlier passage in *IC* IV 41 col. VII runs:

$$[\mu\epsilon\nu o s _____]$$

$$\cdot\cdot]\nu[\cdot\cdot\cdot\cdot\cdot\cdot\cdot\cdot]\tau\alpha\iota\ \kappa\text{-}$$
$$\rho\acute{\eta}\nu\mu\alpha\tau\alpha\ \acute{\epsilon}\pi\grave{\iota}\ \nu\alpha\grave{o}\nu\ \acute{\epsilon}\pi\iota\text{-}$$
$$\delta\iota\acute{o}\mu\epsilon\nu[o\nu]\ \mathring{\eta}\ \acute{\epsilon}\pi\epsilon\lambda\epsilon\acute{\upsilon}\sigma\text{-}$$
$$\alpha\nu\tau\alpha\ \mathring{\eta}\ \theta[\cdot\cdot\cdot\cdot\cdot]\sigma\tau\alpha[$$
$$\cdot]\ \lambda o[\cdot\cdot\cdot]\alpha[\cdot\cdot]\ \pi\epsilon\pi\hat{\alpha}\theta\alpha\iota \qquad 5$$
$$\tau o\upsilon\tau o\nu\ [\cdot\cdot\cdot\cdot\cdot]\iota\alpha[\cdot\cdot$$
$$\cdot]\pi\epsilon[\cdot\cdot]\cdot\alpha\iota\ [\tau\grave{o}]\mu\ \pi\rho\iota\acute{\alpha}\mu\text{-}$$
$$\epsilon\nu o\nu\ [\tau o\hat{\iota}s\ \mu\epsilon\mu\pi]o[\mu\acute{\epsilon}\text{-}$$
$$\nu o\iota s\ \tau\bar{o}\nu]\ \kappa\rho\eta\mu\acute{\alpha}\tau\bar{o}\nu\ \tau\grave{\alpha}\nu$$
$$\ddot{\alpha}\tau\alpha\nu\ \kappa\alpha\tau[\iota]\varsigma\sigma\tau\acute{\alpha}[\mu]\eta\nu\ \ddot{\alpha}\text{-} \qquad 10$$
$$\iota]\ \digamma\epsilon\kappa\acute{\alpha}\sigma\tau\bar{o}\ \acute{\epsilon}\gamma\rho\alpha\tau\tau\alpha\iota,\ \kappa\text{-}$$
$$\alpha\grave{\iota}\ \tau\grave{o}\nu\ \ddot{\alpha}\nu\delta\rho'\ \alpha\grave{\upsilon}\tau\grave{o}\nu\ \acute{\epsilon}\pi\grave{\iota}$$

τοῖς [μ]εμπομένοις τ-
ὸν κρημάτον ἦμην, αἴ κ-
α μὴ περαιόσει ἦ κα πρία-          15
ται ἐν ταῖς τριάκοντ' ἀμέ-
ραις. αἰ δὲ κα συνγνόντι τ-
ἀν δέκ' ἀμερᾶν μὴ περαιόσ-
η]ν, ἀνδοκὰν δὲ καὶ

A rough translation of the relatively complete section, lines 7 ff., might be:

. . . the man who purchased (a slave) is to make good the damage of the articles to the complainants as is written of each (article?), and the man[9] himself is to be in the power of (*epi*) the complainants of the articles, if (the purchaser) does not rescind the agreement, from when he shall have purchased, in the thirty days. But if they (i.e. the vendor and purchaser of the slave) should agree within the ten days not to rescind the agreement and surety also . . .

This is to be set against a short passage in the relevant section of the Great Code (*IC* IV 72 col. VII 10–15):

If someone has bought a slave from the market-place and has not terminated the agreement within sixty days, the one who has acquired him shall be liable, if (the slave) has done any wrong before or after (the purchase).

Placed as it is, as one of three short sections (Willetts 1967: 34. 12–14; Gagarin 1982: 131, sect. 31. 18–20) sandwiched between two long ones, on the sale and mortgage of family property (Willetts 1967: 34. 11; Gagarin 1982: 131,sect. 31, (17)) and on heiresses (Willetts 1967: 34. 15; Gagarin 1982: 131, sect. 31, (21)), it looks again like a piece of generalized case law. However, I remain wholly uncertain whether the provision in the Great Code (*IC* IV 72) was conceived independently of the provisions In *IC* IV 41 col. VII, or is an amendment to them. In the latter case it presumably extended the period in which it was permissible to rescind the contract, in the same way (but without cross-reference) as the provisions of *IC* IV 41 col. VII themselves refer back to still earlier regulations. What is clear, I think, is that it is very hard to suppose that the two passages represented valid law simultaneously.

My second example under this heading is repetition: virtually

---

[9] Interestingly the word *andra*, 'man' is used here for a slave.

the same text appears on *IC IV* 75A and on *IC IV* 81. The topic, which crops up repeatedly in extant laws, is the taking of goods or property as a pledge, or security for a debt. Here the law specifically deals with goods movable or immobile which have been seized as a pledge, but are claimed by the debtor not to be his. The relevant portions of the texts are:

*IC IV* 75A                    *IC IV* 81

 

 

 

δενδρέον καὶ Ϝοικίας ὀ[···
··]τι τον ὀμόρον ἐννέα οἰ
ἐπάνκιστα πεπαμένοι, ·[··
κα̣λ̣[ἐν δ' ἀντὶ μαιτύρōν δυ-      ···κ]αλὲν δ' ἀντὶ μαιτύρō-
ον πρότριτον τὸν] ἐνεκυρ-        ν δυὸν πρότριτον τὸν ἀπ[··
άκσαντα μ[ετρε̄σιόμενον· α-      ···]σαντα μετρε̄σιόμενο-
ὶ δὲ κα μὲ εἴει] καλίοντι ἀ-      ν· αἰ δὲ κα μὲ εἴει καλίον[τι ἄι
ι ἔγρατται α[ὐτὸς μετρέθō τ-     ἔγρ]αται, αὐτὸς μετρέθō τε
ε καὶ προπōνέτ]ο προτέταρτ-     καὶ προπōνέτō προτέτατ]τον
ον ἀντὶ μαιτύ[ρον δυὸν παρέ-    ἀν]τὶ μαιτυρōν δυὸν παρέμε-
μεν ἐνς ἀγορ]ὰν. ὀμνύμεν δὲ      ν ἐνος ἀγοράν. ὀμνύμε[ν δ-
ἐ μὰν τοῦτο μ[έν ἐστι ἀβλοπί-    ἐ ἐ] μὰν τοῦτό μέν ἐστι ἀβλο-
αι δικαίος πρὶν] μōλέσθαι τ-      πίαι δικαίος πρὶν μōλέσθ[αι
[ὰν δίκαν, ὀ δ' ἐνεκύρακσαν]     τὰν] δίκαν, ὃ δ' ἐνεκύρακσαν
[μὲ ἔμεν ————————]          μὲ ἔμεν· νικὲν δ'ὄτερά κ'οἰ π̣[λί
                                   ες ὀ]μόσοντι. vac.

A rough translation of the common portion might be:

(concerning?) trees and house (if?) nine of the neighbours possessing land nearest by swear, [let the lawsuit go forward?]: but he is to summon three days beforehand in the presence of two witnesses the counter party [or: the person who has taken the pledge][10] in order to mark off (the property allegedly pledged): but if the latter should not be (present) to his summons, as has been written, let him mark off (the property) himself and let him enjoin upon (the creditor) four days beforehand to appear in the *agora* before two witnesses. They are to swear that (the land) is verily (the property) of the summoner without damage justly before the suit was brought, but the person who took it as pledge (is to swear) that it is not (the summoner's property): whichever way the majority swear is to win the case.

---

[10] 'The counter party', *IC IV* 81, restoring ἀπ[ομολέ]σαντα with Guarducci: or 'the person who has taken the pledge', *IC IV* 75.

Fig. 3 *IC IV 81*

The text clearly deals with third-party actions to settle the questioned ownership of property which a creditor has taken in pledge. The wording is almost identical in the two documents.[11] Candidly, I do not know why we have two parallel texts. The simple answer, looking at the last lines of *IC IV 81* (not reproduced) with its new sentence ending in mid-air, is that it is a duff copy replaced by *IC IV 75*. In spite of an Athenian parallel (*IG I³ 459, 458*) that is not very convincing, if only because the expedient of deletion and overwriting is certainly found in this body of material. A more complex answer is that *IC IV 81* was a singleton regulation, subsequently incorporated word for word into a broader regulation. The format of *IC IV 75* is compatible with that hypothesis, since at least

[11] The participles denoting the creditor in *IC IV 75*A 2-3 and *IC IV 81*. 5-6 are certainly different.

columns ABC (D is beyond hope) are all dealing with the pledge procedure, B listing objects which may not be taken as pledges for debt, and C allowing a proxy to act in pledge-taking. But if that were the case, we should expect *IC* IV 81 to be deleted, either by complete erasure or by the sort of 'cancellation' with pointed chisel marks which we do have attested elsewhere in the Gortyn material, not least by the right-hand column of *IC* IV 81 itself, as Fig. 3 (*IC* IV 81) shows clearly. The second answer is therefore no more attractive that the first. There must be other possible answers, but I cannot think of them.

The final document I adduce is *IC* IV 43, which shows neither overlap nor repetition but is none the less highly indicative of procedure in various ways.

### *IC* IV 43: Text and translation

B
a  Θιοί· τὰν ἐ[ν] Κησκόραι καὶ
τὰν ἐμ Πάλαι πυταλιὰν ἐ̓[[ε]]
δōκαν ἀ πόλις πυτεῦσαι. α-
ἴ τις ταύταν πρίαιτο ἢ κα-
ταθε[ι̂]το, μὴ κατέκεθαι το-
ι πριαμένōι τὰ[ν δ]ναν μηδ-
ὲ [τὰ]ν κα[τά]θεσιν· μηδ' ἐνεκ-
υράδδεν αἰ μὴ ἐπι[μ]ετρ[ῆι] τὰ-
ν ἐπικαρπίαν. vac.

A
a  Αἴ κ' ἄλōς ἀδ-
ίκōς ἐνεκ[υρ-
άκ]σανς μὴ κ-
αρπōσετ[αι, τ-
ὰς τιμὰνς τō-
ν ἐνεκύρōν κ-
αταστασεῖ ἆι
Fεκάστō ἔγρ-
ατται.

b  Θιοί· τō ποταμō αἴ κα κατὰ τὸ
μέττον τὰν ῥοὰν θιθῆι ῥῆν ( κ-
ατὰ τὸ Fὸν αὐτō, θιθεμένōι ἄ-
πατον ἤμην. τὰν δὲ ῥοὰν λείπ-
εν ὄττον κατέκει ἀ ἐπ' ἀγορᾶ-
ι δέπυρα ἢ πλίον, μεῖον δὲ μή.

b  Αἴ κα δōλον ἢ
δōλαν ἀδίκōς
ἐνεκυράκσει
ἢ ἐδύσει ἢ ἀπ[ολ-
ύσεται, ἐκς ἠμ-
ίνας καταστα-
σεῖ ἔ ἆι τōι ἐλ-
ευθέρōι ἔγρα-
τται, τὰ δὲ τρί-
τρα τᾶ[ς] Fήμα-
ς καὶ τᾶς ἀνπιδή-
μας ἄιπερ [τ]ōι ἐ[λευθέρōι.

Aa  If (someone) having unjustly taken a threshing-floor in pledge shall not have gathered the harvest from it, he shall make good the values of the pledges as is written for each.

Ab   If (someone) has unjustly taken in pledge a male slave or female slave, or has taken away (his/her) clothes or ornaments, he shall make good (the loss) as to half of what is written for the free person, but the third parts of (the value of) the clothes and the ornaments as (is written) for the free person.

Ba   Gods. The city gave the orchard/vineyard in Keskora and in Pale to cultivate. If anyone should buy or mortgage this land, neither the purchase nor the mortgage is to lie [i.e. to be valid?]: nor is anyone to take it in pledge unless he measures out the usufruct [i.e. the usufruct may be taken in pledge?].

Bb   Gods. If anyone makes the flow of the river run from the middle of the river towards his own (property), it is without penalty for the person so doing. (He is) to leave the flow as wide as the bridge at the *agora* holds, or more, but not less.

First, its format consists of two columns (Fig. 4) of text of unequal width, each presenting two documents which appear to be complete in themselves. Given the way in which the letters in the right-hand column (col. A) are squashed, particularly towards the bottom, there were clearly physical constraints for the mason laying out the text. It is pretty clear that the two columns were not planned at the same time, though there are no differences in lettering to suggest that two masons were at work, and it is even moot which column was cut first. Also noteworthy are the faintly visible letters across the middle of the stone between Aa and Ab and between Ba and Bb (Fig. 4). They cannot be made to yield sense consistent with the documents published as *IC* IV 43. Though Guarducci seems strangely nonplussed and does not make the comparison, there is no doubt in my mind that we are dealing with a reused stone, an earlier document having been almost totally erased in a way much more clearly visible on the stones which Guarducci publishes as *IC* IV 47 and *IC* IV 48. I mention this because one can interpret such erasure and reuse in two different ways:

1. As a deliberate way of overcoming the difficulty sketched above in respect of *IC* IV 75A and *IC* IV 81, that of ensuring that superseded provisions were not left standing, ready to mislead litigant and judge: or

2. As a means of economizing on the use of prepared surfaces, especially when, as is frequently the case at Gortyn, we are dealing with stones which were already parts of standing structures when

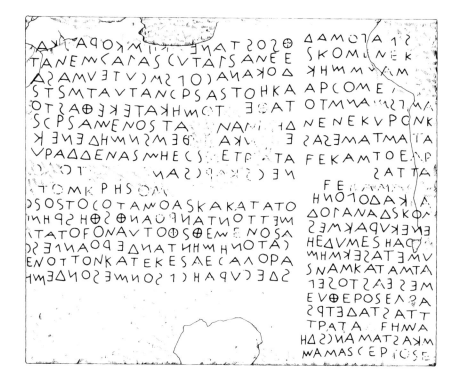

FIG. 4  IC IV 43

the inscriptions they bear were cut, as distinct from the Athenian pattern of creating a new self-standing stele for each new enactment. I do not know which of these explanations is right.

Leaving that question open, the format constrains us to accept that each pair of enactments was seen as belonging together in some sense. Yet, as text and translation show, it is quite unclear in what sense they might belong together. Aa and Ab could indeed be said to be closely linked in subject matter, in that each deals with an aspect of taking something in pledge unjustly and with having to make restitution. Yet that may be a bit superficial, in that each explicitly refers to, and builds on, previously existing written regulations. Certainly neither of them can possibly be seen as a full statement of the law on taking pledges. I would rather take them both as further examples of the sort of item which I discussed above (Sect. 3) on columns XI–XII of the Great Code: formulations emerging from the necessity to sort out actual cases in court which are seen to expose gaps or inequities in existing statutes.

If so, two consequences follow. First, the way they arise makes them into aspects both of untidying existing law, and of providing the raw material of subsequent re-tidying. It is therefore a little unlucky that though col. I of the Great Code (*IC* IV 72) does indeed deal with subject-matter not far away from that of *IC* IV 43 Ab, its main preoccupation is with persons of disputed status, so that we cannot follow the fortunes of the provision at *IC* IV 43 Ab further into recodification. The second consequence is that their collocation in *IC* IV 43 A does not have to be a consequence of their being, as it were, first cousins in subject-matter: it could just as easily result from the chance that the cases which presented these difficulties appeared before the courts at roughly the same period. Certainly the pairing of the two documents in *IC* IV 43 B fits that hypothesis, for they have nothing whatever in common with each other as far as subject-matter goes and can only have been inscribed together if some principle other than subject grouping was at work.

### 5. CONCLUSIONS ON CODIFICATION

The most rapid way of formulating that principle lies via a further question: who promulgated these documents, whether the extended 'codes' such as *IC* IV 41 or *IC* IV 72 or *IC* IV 75, or the smaller items such as *IC* IV 43? Since specific officials such as *nomothetai* ('lawmakers') are conspicuously absent from the list of magistrates at Gortyn (Guarducci 1950: 31–2), good method enjoins the least adventurous hypothesis. It is likely that they were promulgated by the main magistrates, the *kosmoi* and *gnomones* with or without their subordinates the *mnamones* (see Thomas, this volume), for it remains wholly unclear to me whether the person or persons called *dikastai*, 'judges' (*IC* IV 41 col. V; *IC* IV 42B; *IC* IV 72 *passim*), need be anything more than a *kosmos* wearing a judge's wig. However, it would not affect the argument even if the *dikastai* were a separate magistracy, for what matters is that we have to do with office-holders who hold office for a finite term (how long is not known) and may not hold office again until a specified period has elapsed (*IC* IV 14 g–p 2: three years for a *kosmos*, five for a *xenios kosmos*, ten for a *gnomon*). Suppose then that we say the principle of unity behind all the documents which we have been surveying is chronological. That is, each of them, whether big 'code' (*IC* IV 72), little 'codes' (*IC* IV 41 and *IC* IV 75), or minor groupings (*IC* IV 43), is the document issued by (let us say) the relevant magistrates at the end of their period of office setting out the changes in the law which they proposed/instigated/proclaimed/approved during their period of office.

This hypothesis would explain various things. It would explain, for example, (*a*) why the documents vary so much in length. This variation might be related to a number of different factors, for example to the nature of the problems which presented themselves in court, to the political atmosphere, and to the degree to which the board of magistrates in post were dead-beats or had a Lord Denning's creative genius for legal systematization and innovation. It would also explain (*b*) why the same topic can recur in various documents, and why the same document or dossier (I think here of the Great Code, obviously) can include such a spectrum of topics, treated at such varied length and with such a range of difference between (at one extreme) amendments on specific points and (at the other) a thoroughgoing recast of the entire corpus of law on a particular subject. It further explains (*c*) why the Great Code can give a specific starting-date for the validity of a regulation (*IC* IV 72 col.V 4–6: 'when the Aithalian *startos*, Kyllos and his colleagues, were the *kosmoi*'), and (*d*) why, as I have already tried to suggest, amendments to the main body of the Great Code, *IC* IV 72, can themselves be part of *IC* IV 72. Lastly, and fundamentally, it helps to explain why both *IC* IV 72 itself and the rest of the Gortynian legal material show evidence of the two contradictory processes, of codification and one-off amendment/replacement, in equal measure.

However, there are two objections to this hypothesis.[12] Both challenge the twin assumptions, implicit within it, that such inscribed statutes as we have at Gortyn were genuinely meant to guide what the courts did, and were applied in practice. The first objection, based on the texts themselves, is that for all their ostensible detail they were unusable in practice. Cross-references, for

---

[12] Various forms of them were put by members of the seminar and by Dr S. C. Todd. I am most grateful to all concerned.

example,[13] usually in the form 'as is written' (*ai egrattai*), were so unspecific that no one not already fully cognizant of the material could find his way about. Documents are not dated (*IC* IV 72 col.V 1–9 is the sole exception), so that there was no means short of deletion of knowing which provision has superseded which other. The absence of any formula for amendment comparable to the Athenian 'in other respects, in accordance with' (*ta men alla kathaper*) is incompatible with the need for integration and consistency which any mature set of genuinely applicable rules should show. More generally, we cannot be sure that the reason for deletion was to ensure statutory consistency rather than to suppress old social statements in favour of fresh ones which corresponded more closely to current values, prejudices, or ideals—at which point we join the current exploration of law as discourse about the state of society rather than as a set of rules intended to keep the social system working (Humphreys 1988: 465; 1985).

These points are scarcely fatal. The final point embodies a false disjunction, for any legal system must be both, while no one will deny that the extant material reflects intense social debate, especially about the details of inheritance and about the taking of pledges as security for debts. The other points apply not so much to the intention of the lawmaking and recording process as to its competence. Limited though the cross-reference technique was, it was probably an adequate *aide-mémoire* for the *kosmos* or *dikastas* concerned, and indeed showed more sophistication that was lacking in Athenian documentation, then or later, with consequences in the form of muddle, overlap, and contradiction which Nikomachos and his colleagues had to face (see Todd, this volume). Likewise the procedure for amendment, on my view deriving from 'case-law', may have been clumsy and may have failed to integrate new regulations with the main body of law. But it was more workable with a single judge[14] known to be responsible, who needed his decisions validated and protected, than it would have been in a system administered by mass juries. Indeed, one may go further and observe, first, that texts such as *IC* IV 72 cols. V 1–9, IX 16, XI 19–23, and XII 1–5, specifying that this or that provision is to be

---

[13] *IC* IV 72 cols. IV 30–1, VI 31, IX 23–4, XI 27–9, XII 1–5, leaving aside cols. IV 45–6, 48, 50–1 and cols. VIII 29–30, 35–6, 40 as being internal cross-references. Apart from the Great Code, cf. also *IC* IV 56.

[14] Plus assessors, if Kyllos' *startos* really had that function.

valid from year X, or from the inscription of the law, make sense only in a context of practicality, and, second, that laws were not worth changing if they were not the actual basis of judgement or decision.

The second objection, based on comparative evidence, would be more subversive if sustained. One major strand in the study of the great Mesopotamian codes has been a growing willingness to entertain the idea that they are not, as they purport to be, codified statute law, or a collection of decisions on the facts of a number of cases, or even practical guidance for judges, so much as a literary creation whereby the king presents himself, retrospectively, as he wishes to be seen.[15] Without testing the idea in depth, for which I lack any expertise, we may still ask if the hypothesis is worth transferring to Gortyn. Hardly so, for two reasons. First, neither the extremely high level of detail throughout the documentation, nor the concentration on socially edgy areas of law, nor the heterogeneity of topic within the same 'document', encourages the idea that specifically literary norms were paramount. Secondly, there is no identifiable person or group whose glory is magnified by these texts. Even if Kyllos and his colleagues did draft the Great Code (*IC* IV 72), they are hardly prominent therein, while otherwise, with the shadowy exception of Thaletas (Guarducci 1950: 18–19), the lawyers of Gortyn are singularly anonymous.

We are left, therefore, with a hypothesis: that the legal material from Gortyn is real and shows two contradictory processes, that of codification or systematization, and that of continuous amendment or decodification via generalized case-law, in operation at the same time. Legal historians familiar with the English common law should find no difficulty therein: all it need do is to warn us against using the word 'code' too easily.

---

[15] Main references: Kraus (1960); Finkelstein (1961); Bottéro (1982). References to other comparative material can be found in Humphreys (1988: 483 n. 2).

# 4

# Oaths and Dispute Settlement in Ancient Greek Law

## GERHARD THÜR

### 1. INTRODUCTION

As a lawyer I feel a little uncomfortable when addressing historians. Our common interest is, generally speaking, human behaviour. The historian is interested in its descriptive aspect, 'as it is or was', the lawyer in a normative one, 'as it ought to be' (cf. Foxhall, this volume). A legal historian falls between the two stools; my field of study is law as part of everyday life in Greek antiquity—'law as it was'. Naturally I am also concerned with the ideas the ancient Greeks had about what law ought to be. One might expect to find such ideas in the writings of the Greek philosophers, but in fact the Greek philosophers never considered everyday legal problems in the ways ancient Roman jurists did and modern jurists continue to do. Consequently one has to reconstruct both the details and the principles of Greek law by studying every available source: literature (including philosophy), inscriptions, papyri—evaluating every piece of evidence in its special local and temporal context. The so-called legal texts—laws (*nomoi*), contracts, judgements, and forensic speeches—are no more significant than epic, lyric, tragic, or historiographic writings. References to the principles of Greek law as an everyday phenomenon may be found in all sorts of statements of ancient Greek contemporaries. From the beginning of this century legal historians, particularly Ernst Rabel and Hans Julius Wolff, have emphasized that modern legal categories are not adequate tools with which to understand ancient Greek legal sources.

To reveal the disguised structures of individual human communities is the common task of both legal history and anthropology. Why should they not be combined? Louis Gernet, who was above

all a superb classicist, achieved it very successfully. Efforts are now
being made by David Cohen and Michael Gagarin, in very different
ways, and also by Uwe Wesel. Some of these adopt approaches
which appear to me to be dangerous. There is in particular a risk
in turning to anthropological analysis before all the evidence of the
Greek sources has been exhausted. It is easier to consult an anthropological textbook for quick information than dozens of Greek
lexicons and indexes, even if these are computerized. Similarly,
comparative legal history, for instance the ancient Near Eastern
cuneiform law, is increasingly ignored. Serious legal anthropology
in the field of ancient Greek law must, therefore, be kept within reasonable bounds, whilst home-made and second-hand anthropology
must be kept outside them. What is required for legal history is first-
hand discussion between the two disciplines.

I am first going to deconstruct some reconstructions of legal procedure in Homeric times. Dispute-settlement theories are closely
linked to theories on the beginnings of the state, the *polis*. Here too
some ideas need to be deconstructed. Secondly I will try to reconstruct early Greek dispute settlement in a more convincing manner,
but whether this should lead to a reconstruction of the origins of
the *polis* is beyond my purpose here.

## 2. DECONSTRUCTION

The central sources to be discussed are Homer, *Iliad* 23 and 18, the
law of Drakon, and the code of Gortyn, ranging from 700 to 450
BC. Before considering these texts, however, I will summarize the
three main streams of interpretation which have held sway during
the last hundred years. Until 1946 the common opinion was as follows: in order to settle disputes in prehistoric times individuals
could voluntarily waive self-help and resort to arbitration.
Gradually, under the influence of public opinion, the litigants were
deprived of the use of private force and compelled to submit their
disputes to the authorities. The leaders of the primitive community
were determined on as the arbitrators. After the consolidation of
the state, this jurisdiction became a legal institution and passed
from the early monarchs to aristocratic city magistrates before
finally falling to the popular courts. What a wonderfully evolutionary picture! The main authority is Homer, *Iliad* 18. 501: 'and each
desired to win the case on the word of an *istor*' (ἄμφω δ' ἱέσθην ἐπὶ

ἵστορι πεῖραρ ἐλέσθαι), where *istor* is understood to mean 'arbitrator'.[1]

In a pioneering article Wolff (1946) objected that it seemed unlikely that a mere tendency towards arbitration would have been sufficient for successfully suppressing anarchy. If, on the other hand, such a success had been achieved, why should the state have troubled to put its authority behind a working system of private arbitration? Further, Wolff drew attention to the fact that everywhere in the Greek *polis* self-help had existed for a long time even up to the historic period. In his opinion the princes had never acted as arbitrators. They ensured social peace by granting an accused person a kind of temporary 'police protection' from acts of revenge. The princes, as public authorities, controlled self-help; after examining the legal position they would either permit or prevent recourse to self-help. Wolff supposed a direct development from Homeric times to the classical *polis*. In his opinion the *istor* of *Iliad* 18. 501 is not an arbitrator but a person with direct knowledge of the facts who is a means of bringing about an immediate decision.

Wolff's theory won considerable support amongst legal historians. The first objection was raised by a philologist, Hildebrecht Hommel (1969).[2] For Hommel *Iliad* 18. 501 can only be understood as a voluntary submission to arbitration. In the Homeric *polis* disputes were settled by compromise; each litigant had to meet his opponent half-way. They both had to choose from amongst several settlements proposed by the elders (*gerontes*). The dispute was settled when the litigants both accepted one of the proffered settlements. In 1970 I made some, apparently ineffective, objections to Hommel's theory (Thür 1970; cf. now, Thür 1989 and 1990). How can the method of dispute settlement he assumes work if each plaintiff compromises whether right or wrong, and more or less automatically obtains a half of what he demands, for simultaneously the defendant loses to the same extent? My proposed solution, differing from both Wolff and Hommel, was that normally disputes were settled by decisory oaths. Further discussion, by amongst others Talamanca (1979), has followed this particular path.

Recently two scholars, Gagarin (1986) and Stahl (1987), have

---

[1] Hesiod, *Works and Days* 35-6, is taken to represent an intermediate stage of 'obligatory arbitration' found especially in Boeotian society.

[2] Hommel (1928) first advanced this view; see now van Effenterre (1994) and Thür (1994).

independently returned to Hommel's arbitration theory. The main difference from Hommel is that neither relies on nineteenth-century evolutionary models but rather upon anthropology: forced by public opinion, litigants voluntarily submitted their dispute to the elders of Homeric society. Jointly both litigants chose one of the proposed settlements to decide the dispute. Gagarin (1986: 20) understands this arbitration to be a 'formal, public procedure', whilst Stahl calls it a 'pre-state procedure' (1987: 167)—the difference seems merely a matter of definition. Gagarin may have in some ways the better case, but I do not want to insist on this. More important is the manner in which both deal with the question of the oaths.

Gagarin discovered some examples of oaths of denial. In his list of eight main elements of procedure in what he calls 'pre-written-law society', oaths figure as number 6: 'an oath of denial may be sworn or asked for by one of the parties, though this oath does not necessarily decide the case' (1986: 43). One should note, though, that a lawyer only speaks of an 'oath of denial' or exculpatory oath when the defendant is automatically exonerated by swearing it. Gagarin is correct to say that no early literary source explicitly states that a certain oath, if sworn, will be decisive. He gives only one example of an oath of denial sworn by a defendant and, as he says, this does not settle the case (1986: 40). But this is not at all conclusive. In the *Homeric Hymn to Hermes* the new-born god does not swear the great oath of innocence as Gagarin implies but is only said to be ready to swear it (4. 383). Hermes clearly does not interrupt his speech for a swearing ceremony. So we may ignore Gagarin's non-decisive oath of denial.

Stahl (1987: 166, 168) explains the oaths of his 'pre-state procedure' in another way: as in classical Athens, in the earlier procedure each party had to swear a preliminary oath. Consequently, these two opposite oaths sworn at the commencement of an arbitration could by no means be decisive. But Stahl is not able to provide a single piece of evidence for such preliminary oaths in Homer. I shall demonstrate later that the double oath is nothing other than a relatively late institution created especially to avoid the decisory oath taken by one litigant only. It is very unlikely to date back to Homeric times.

To sum up, Wolff's argument that there is no development from Homer to the self-help in the later Greek *polis* is conclusive against the various theories based upon arbitration. Furthermore, the proposition that in *Iliad* 18 the litigants themselves jointly choose a settlement from amongst several proposed has no parallel in legal anthropology. So far as I can see, Tiv litigants—quoted by Gagarin (1986: 31) as his best comparative example—go around from one elder to another until they find a convenient person, not a settlement. Just as unconvincing are the 'big men' cited by Stahl (1987: 169—without a source; perhaps a quotation derived third-hand from Wesel).[3] On the other hand Wolff's theory that in early Greek society the authorities granted the defendant temporary police protection has no better support. In later times sanctuaries protected accused persons by giving them asylum, and, as mythology teaches, this was an old custom.

### 3. RECONSTRUCTION

I now proceed to adduce evidence for a better theory, which goes further than my previous attempt. First I shall briefly summarize. Voluntary resort to arbitration or compromise did no doubt play an important part in early Greek society and later on as well. If no peaceful agreement could be achieved the prosecutor was allowed to use private force against his opponent; but before he was allowed to do so some authority had to decide in a formal procedure whether self-help was legal or not in that case. In democratic Athens the magistrates brought the cases before a popular court. By voting the defendant guilty the jurors opened the way for the private use of force. In contrast, in early Greece magistrates did not decide cases themselves. Rather they would formulate an oath and decide which of the litigants was to submit to taking it. This—as I shall show—is the meaning of *dikazein* ('to decide'). *Dikazein* in fact means to swear to the facts of the case by an appropriate deity, sometimes with the addition of sanctions for falsity. If the oath was successfully taken the party swearing won the case and no further judgement was necessary. Technically I call this type of judgement a *Beweisurteil*, for which the term 'medial judgement' has been used in analysis of the early common law. It is so called because

---

[3] Gagarin is generalizing his model. But starting from his own premisses, there could never be an unjust judgement of the kind of which Hesiod (*Works and Days* 219, 250), for example, speaks. How can a judgement be 'crooked' if either party is free to reject it?

the magistrate does not decide on guilt or innocence but only gives
a judgement about the oath-formula which, if taken, will automatically resolve the dispute. Wolff understood *dikazein* differently:
the authorities 'allowed or forbad self-help' after a formal proof. In
my opinion, self-help was not controlled by police protection or any
question of permission or prohibition by any authorities. A prosecutor was only allowed to use private force after he had obtained
divine legitimation by an oath. Punishment by an offended god was
a real threat to people in archaic times.

What evidence can be provided for my theory that oaths played
a substantial part in early Greek dispute settlement? Before discussing the earliest sources it might be of some interest to ask how
Greek authors of the fourth century BC saw their own legal history.
Both Plato and Aristotle wrote about early dispute settlement. One
must keep in mind, however, that in their time *dikazein* was used
merely for the verdict given by a popular court. No Athenian magistrate was competent to *dikazein* a lawsuit. Terminology and principles of legal procedure certainly had changed during the 350
years since Homer. Did fourth-century writers know more about it
than we do? Clearly they knew a lot, but they may have misunderstood much also.

The source generally considered the most important is Aristotle,
*Constitution of the Athenians* 3. 5 (but cf. also *Politics* 1298ᵃ9-31):

κύριοι δ' ἦσαν καὶ τὰς δίκας αὐτοτελεῖς κρίνειν καὶ οὐχ ὥσπερ νῦν
προανακρίνειν.

They also had the power to give final judgement in lawsuits and not as
now merely to hold a preliminary trial.

In the fourth century BC there were two stages leading to a verdict
by a popular court: first, the litigants had to meet before a magistrate in a preliminary session, called *anakrisis* (examination) or
*prodikasia* (preliminary hearing)—Aristotle combines both words in
a neologism *proanakrinein* (preliminary examination); second, the
litigants pleaded before a popular court of at least 200 jurors, who
gave their verdict by voting simply 'yes' or 'no'. Before Drakon,
Aristotle says—and modern scholarship agrees with him—the
Athenian archons (magistrates) had the authority to settle disputes
within their own competence: *krinein* (to decide). Solon was the first
to introduce the decision by a popular court, the Heliaia. But to me

it seems suspicious that Aristotle does not use the word *dikazein* which we find in the law of Drakon (*IG* I³ 104. 10-11); furthermore a law of Solon entitles the archons to act as *dikastai*, judges' (Demosthenes 23. 28). So we should expect to find *dikazein* in Aristotle too. It seems probable that some of the detail given by Aristotle is also misleading.

In the third book of his *Politics* (1285ᵇ9-12) Aristotle is dealing with the monarchy. In ancient times, he says, kings also gave judgements in lawsuits; *krinein* ('to decide') again.

κύριοι δ' ἦσαν τῆς τε κατὰ πόλεμον ἡγεμονίας καὶ τῶν θυσιῶν ὅσαι μὴ ἱερατικαί, καὶ πρὸς τούτοις τὰς δίκας ἔκρινον· τοῦτο δ' ἐποίουν οἱ μὲν οὐκ ὀμνύοντες οἱ δ' ὀμνύοντες, ὁ δ' ὅρκος ἦν τοῦ σκήπτρου ἐπανάτασις.

And they held the supreme command in war and had control over all sacrifices not in the hands of the priests and moreover decided lawsuits; some gave judgement without an oath some on oath, the oath was taken by holding up a sceptre.

Here the philosopher goes into some detail. Judgement is said to be given partly on oath. Such an oath taken by a judge is known only from a single archaic Greek source, the law code of Gortyn (*IC* IV 72), e.g. col. I 17-24:

αἰ δέ κ' ἀνπὶ δόλοι μολίοντι πονίοντες Ϝὸν Ϝεκάτερος ἔμεν, αἰ μὲν κα μαίτυς ἀποπονêι, κατὰ τὸν μαίτυρα δικάδδεν, αἰ δέ κ' ἒ ἀνποτέροις ἀποπονίοντι ἒ μεδατέροι, τὸν δικαστὰν ὀμνύντα κρίνεν.

And if they are in dispute about a slave each declaring that it is his, the judge is to give judgement according to the witness, if there be witness but the decision is to be on oath if the evidence be for both or for neither.

The Cretan *dikastas* (judge) belongs to the board of supreme magistrates, the *kosmoi*. In matters uncertain or of minor importance he is allowed to decide the case by giving a judgement on oath: *omnynta krinein* (I 21-4). If there are good witnesses on one side or the case is more important the magistrate has to give a *dikazein*, judgement (I 18-21). Aristotle, above, may be referring to an archaic system of legal procedure like that of Gortyn. In the very next line he calls the king *dikastes*, judge. The parallels in Gortyn suggest that *omnyon krinein* 'to give judgement on oath' is but a subsidiary way of settling disputes. In the usual way judgements are 'not on oath', the *dikazein* which Aristotle never mentions.

Although Plato does not use the verb *dikazein*, in one passage in

the *Laws* (948b) he gives an exact account of it. Until now this evidence has been ignored. The mythical king Rhadamanthys made
short work of disputes: he imposed an oath on the litigants and so
disposed of the matter. Because in his time people did not commit
perjury his method succeeded. In the following lines Plato complains that in his own time both litigants had to swear, so that in
every lawsuit there must necessarily be one perjurer. Consequently
in his state Plato forbids the double preliminary oath. Rhadamanthys must therefore have imposed an oath on only one party.
Dispute settlement by imposing a decisive oath is well known from
the law code of Gortyn. Lines III 1-12 forbid a divorcee to carry
away anything belonging to the husband. If there was a dispute the
*dikastas* had to impose on her an oath of denial (III 5-9). Artemis,
whom women had reason to fear above all, was the deity competent to guarantee her oath. The verb used here is *dikazein*: the magistrate decrees what kind of oath has to be taken and which of the
litigants or whose witnesses have to take it and what the consequences should be. It is not unlikely that Plato had similar ideas
about the judgements of Rhadamanthys. He might have avoided
using the verb *dikazein* because his fellow Athenians were likely to
understand it as referring to the verdict given by the popular court,
the *dikasterion*. Significantly, the Platonic myth seems to offer better evidence of Heroic times than the scholarly efforts of Aristotle.[4]

The crucial texts, however, are the dispute between Antilochos
and Menelaos and the lawsuit depicted on the famous shield of
Achilles, *Iliad* 23. 573-85 and 18. 497-508 respectively. In both
cases we find dispute settlement by *dikazein*. On the basis of my earlier considerations one may supplement the wordless scene pictured
on the shield with the epic narrative of the other.

> ἀλλ' ἄγετ', Ἀργείων ἡγήτορες ἠδὲ μέδοντες,
> ἐς μέσον ἀμφοτέροισι δικάσσατε, μηδ' ἐπ' ἀρωγῇ,
> μή ποτέ τις εἴπῃσιν Ἀχαιῶν χαλκοχιτώνων·      575
> Ἀντίλοχον ψεύδεσσι βιησάμενος Μενέλαος
> οἴχεται ἵππον ἄγων, ὅτι οἱ πολὺ χείρονες ἦσαν
> ἵπποι, αὐτὸς δὲ κρείσσων ἀρετῇ τε βίῃ τε.

---

[4] I draw attention in passing to King Minos, Rhadamnathys' colleague. In the
*Odyssey* (11. 569-71) we find him 'laying down the law', *themisteuein*. Neither
*dikazein* nor oaths are mentioned. But he is holding the sceptre like the other authorities who *dikazoun*.

εἰ δ' ἄγ' ἐγὼν αὐτὸς δικάσω, καί μ' οὔ τινά φημι
ἄλλον ἐπιπλήξειν Δαναῶν· ἰθεῖα γὰρ ἔσται.          580
Ἀντίλοχ', εἰ δ' ἄγε δεῦρο, διοτρεφές, ἧ θέμις ἐστί,
στὰς ἵππων προπάροιθε καὶ ἄρματος, αὐτὰρ ἱμάσθλην
χερσὶν ἔχε ῥαδινήν, ἧ περ τὸ πρόσθεν ἔλαυνες,
ἵππων ἁψάμενος γαιήοχον ἐννοσίγαιον
ὄμνυθι μὴ μὲν ἑκὼν τὸ ἐμὸν δόλῳ ἄρμα πεδῆσαι.          585

Come now, ye leaders and rulers of the Argives,
judge aright betwixt us twain having regard to neither
lest later some of the brazen-coated Achaeans say:
'Over Antilochos did Menelaos prevail by lies,
and left with the mare for though his horses were the worse he himself was
mightier in worth and power.'
But I myself will decide rightly and none of the Danaans will reproach me
for my judgement will be straight.
Antilochos, come forward, beloved of Zeus, as is customary, stand before
thy horses and chariot taking the whip wherewith you did drive and laying thy hand upon the horses swear by the holder and shaker of the earth
that
not of thine own will did thou hinder my horses by guile.

Antilochos had overtaken Menelaos in the chariot race by means
of a foul trick. In the presence of the Achaean assembly Menelaos
claims the second prize, a mare, of which Antilochos has taken possession. Menelaos, sceptre in hand, addresses the other kings. Most
striking in this speech is that Menelaos first asks the leaders to give
judgement (*dikazein*) and then gives a judgement (*dikazein*) himself
in his own cause. For this reason Wolff regards the controversy as
remaining throughout within the context of self-help. Gagarin and
Stahl do not like these two references to *dikazein* at all. They each
stress that the episode as a whole is an illustration of dispute settlement by compromise. However, at the start we have quite a normal lawsuit. The *dikazein* of Menelaos is irrefutable: he formulates
an oath, which everybody would regard as the correct way to settle a dispute about a chariot race. Poseidon is to charioteers and
their horses what Artemis is to women. Perjury would be dangerous, Poseidon would not allow a perjurer further success in chariot racing. So Antilochos gave in and did not risk the god's
punishment. The judgement 'Antilochos is to swear' would have
been the result of the session, since none of the other leaders had
'blamed' Menelaos (l. 580). Such blame could have prompted a

new *dikazein*, judgement: for instance that Menelaos was to swear
rather than Antilochos. But Antilochos at once withdrew, so
Menelaos' judgement remained at the stage of a proposal. To sum
up, the two *dikazein* in this text seem to harmonize best if we
assume that the other leaders formulated oaths too, as Menelaos
did. An oath according to the *dikazein* sworn by one of the litigants
would have settled the dispute. The best parallel is the *dikazein*,
judgement, in the law code of Gortyn (ll. III 5–9).

In the shield scene we find *dikazein* in line 506 and *diken eipein*
(to propose judgement) in line 508. We are not told of one word
spoken by the judges, but we can witness the scene.

> λαοὶ δ' εἰν ἀγορῇ ἔσαν ἀθρόοι· ἔνθα δὲ νεῖκος
> ὠρώρει, δύο δ' ἄνδρες ἐνείκεον εἵνεκα ποινῆς
> ἀνδρὸς ἀποκταμένου· ὁ μὲν εὔχετο πάντ' ἀποδοῦναι
> δήμῳ πιφαύσκων, ὁ δ' ἀναίνετο μηδὲν ἑλέσθαι·            500
> ἄμφω δ' ἱέσθην ἐπὶ ἴστορι πεῖραρ ἑλέσθαι.
> λαοὶ δ' ἀμφοτέροισιν ἐπήπυον, ἀμφὶς ἀρωγοί.
> κήρυκες δ' ἄρα λαὸν ἐρήτυον· οἱ δὲ γέροντες
> ἥατ' ἐπὶ ξεστοῖσι λίθοις ἱερῷ ἐνὶ κύκλῳ,
> σκῆπτρα δὲ κηρύκων ἐν χέρσ' ἔχον ἠεροφώνων·           505
> τοῖσιν ἔπειτ' ἤϊσσον, ἀμοιβηδὶς δὲ δίκαζον.
> κεῖτο δ' ἄρ' ἐν μέσσοισι δύο χρυσοῖο τάλαντα,
> τῷ δόμεν ὃς μετὰ τοῖσι δίκην ἰθύντατα εἴποι.

But the people were gathered in the assembly place, for there strife stirred,
for two men struggled over the blood-price of a man slain, the one
entreated that he had paid everything, proclaiming to the community, but
the other refused to take anything; and each desired to win the case on the
word of an *istor*. And the people cheered both, being supporters of each
side in turn. But the heralds restrained the people. And the elders sat on
polished rocks in the sacred circle, and they held in their hands the sceptres of the loud-voiced heralds. Then they would dart out and give judgement (*dikazon*), each in turn. And there lay in the middle two talents of
gold, to give to whoever among them should speak the straightest judgement (*dike*).

Two men have brought their dispute before the assembly of the
elders sitting in a sacred circle in the agora. Most probably the issue
is whether the defendant had paid blood money or not. After the
litigants have pleaded, some elders, holding their sceptres, stand up
and give their judgements. An award is to be made for that elder
who speaks *dike*, the straightest way. I will discuss three questions

only: (1) who wins the award (ll. 507–8)? (2) what is the meaning of *dikazein* (l. 506) here? and (3) who is the famous *istor* (literally 'one who knows') of line 501?

1. We are on relatively firm ground in answering the first question. Larsen (1949) has shown that in Homeric assemblies the leaders went on discussing a problem until no further objections were made and one proposal prevailed. Gagarin (1986: 31, 36) provides some anthropological parallels. We do not need Hommel's artificial solution that the litigants themselves jointly designated the winner.

2. The meaning of *dikazein* is more speculative. In order to maintain his theory of arbitration Gagarin constructs some sophisticated issues the litigants might have been quarrelling about. He cannot imagine how on such a simple question as whether a *poine* (sum of blood money) has been paid or not there could be any competition between the elders of the city. Gagarin thinks nobody pays except in the presence of witnesses. In my opinion only the most simple events harmonize with the idyll of peaceful life Hephaistos modelled on the shield. Considering line 499: 'the one entreated that he had paid everything', dispute may have arisen for instance about some of a number of beasts, the usual fine for killing. Some of them may have been sick or stolen property, or have run back to their former owner, or perhaps payment might simply have been partly postponed. No dramatic issue at all, but amongst peasants reason enough for a quarrel. More serious is the question how could the elders compete in giving the best answer if the dispute admitted of only two, alternative, answers? Wolff's suggestion that much depends on the reasoning given for each solution cannot satisfy. For me, it seems best to follow the meaning of *dikazein* discussed above: the elders formulated different oaths, each trying to reflect most appropriately the details of this particular case. The question whether the fine was paid or not admits of only two answers. But the elders were not concerned to answer this question at all. They simply competed for the best way to find the right answer. More exactly, their problem was which of the litigants should swear and to what form of oath? In the same way Menelaus proposed an oath about a question in the alterative: should he or Antilochos carry away the mare? Here several oath-formulations were possible; one leader may blame the other. The shield scene makes clear that

oaths are proposed until one is indisputably accepted. This is the 'straightest' way to settle the dispute.

3. Up to this point my interpretation has found no room for the *istor*. There is a general assumption that he is to be found amongst the elders: the *istor* will be the one who wins the award. That each litigant resorted to the *istor* is by no means an argument for voluntary submission to arbitration. Wolff correctly pointed out that the same words would be spoken within a context of public control over self-help. There was no other way for the defendant to obtain protection or for the plaintiff to obtain permission to resort to private force than to go before the authorities. If litigants of today say 'let's go to law' nobody thinks in terms of voluntary arbitration. So the solution depends upon the meaning of the word *istor* itself. Gagarin's translation 'arbiter' relies on *Iliad* 23. 450-98, a passage he has clearly misunderstood. In the chariot race Ideomeneos and Ajax disagree as to who is in first place at the moment. Ideomeneos proposes laying a bet on it and appointing Agamemnon as *istor* (23. 486-7). Gagarin (1986: 37 n. 37) says: 'Presumably Agamemnon would decide the outcome of the race.' In my opinion there is nothing to decide: in the event everybody will be able to observe who is actually first. Agamemnon's only task will have been to hold the stake money and hand it over to the winner. Therefore he does not have to act as arbitrator, rather he is a guarantor for the bet's being enforced correctly. In some accord with the meaning 'guarantor' is the scholion to line 486 (Maas 427): *istora] synthekophylaka* (depositary of a contract). Indeed, on inscriptions from Boeotia of the third century BC there is mention of *istores* at the end of private documents. But these do not, of course, explain the *istor* on the shield of Achilles.

Wolff relies on etymology: *istor* is an expert, the one who knows. Nevertheless his theory that the elder winning the award decides the case 'on the ground of (his) knowledge of the facts involved' seems to be far-fetched. Nowhere else in Greek law do we have parallels to the Anglo-Saxon jury Wolff presumes to find in Homer.

My solution is to disassociate the *istor* from the elder winning the award. If the winning elder has to formulate a decisive oath, *diken eipein* or *dikazein* cannot be the end of the trial. Only when the oath which has been formulated is taken is the dispute between the parties settled. Consequently, the *peirar*, the end (l. 501), must follow the *dikazein* and take place beyond the scene depicted on the shield. None of the elders is to be identified with the *istor*. Rather I would suggest linking the *istor* of line 501 with the *istores* known as gods who 'witness', that is to say guarantee, archaic oaths. Examples are the famous Athenian ephebic oath (Lykourgos 1. 77; cf. Tod 1948: 204) and the Hippocratic oath. The *istor* in the shield scene is none other than the deity or deities by whom the litigants are going to swear. Having pleaded their case (l. 499-500) each litigant has asked the elders to award him an oath, the exact wording of which he has suggested.

Litigants' resorting to oaths commonly occurs as a theme in epic literature. Hermes, for instance, offered an oath of denial: 'I did not drive the cows to my house' (*Homeric Hymns* 4. 379 ff.). Because he had hidden them in a cave the oath could have been truthfully sworn. But it is a good example of a 'crooked *dike*' of the type we later find in Hesiod. On the contrary, the *dikazein* of Menelaos is certainly a 'straight *dike*' (*Iliad* 23. 580). From the shield scene we learn that each party proposes an oath favourable to his own position. The elders have to decide which of them is 'straight' and may even propose 'straighter' ones; the 'straightest' will win the award. The Hermes story makes clear that in such a system of litigation much can depend on a single word. Generally people will not have wished to perjure themselves. But their relations with the gods were very formal. A screwed but true oath would not result in harm. To settle disputes, the authorities of the early *polis* must have kept in their minds a considerable repertory of oath formulae. Beyond that they required great skill to adapt them to particular situations. During the negotiations to find the straightest oath a litigant must often have seen his case disappear. Like Antilochos, many others will have resorted to compromise. Dispute settlement by imposing a decisory oath strongly encouraged peaceable agreement.

Leaving aside Aristotle I have followed a trail leading back from the Platonic myth of Rhadamanthys, where I found a decision made by imposing an oath, to the law code of Gortyn, where in the fifth century BC this procedure was practised and labelled *dikazein*, and finally to the two crucial Homeric texts. Neither voluntary arbitration nor control of self-help by police power was the principle of early Greek dispute settlement, rather control by supernatural means, by the imposition of decisive oaths. The authority of the leaders consists in their exclusive competence to utter the correct formulae for these oaths.

These findings are by no means surprising. Ries (1989) has recently published a detailed survey of early Babylonian medial judgements. In the cuneiform documents he finds two types of judgement: only if the defendant confessed his guilt or the plaintiff produced documentary evidence would the lawcourt immediately give its verdict. Normally a judgement imposed on one of the parties was a decisory oath to be sworn some time later in a sanctuary. Oriental influence on the early Greek *polis* is not impossible; the well-known *Beweisurteil* of the old German customary procedure, on the other hand, suggests the possibility of independent parallel development.

By way of conclusion I will summarize the advantages and disadvantages of this system, which was finally transformed either as democratic jurisdiction as in Athens or within aristocratic models as, for example, in Gortyn.

Hesiod's *Works and Days* deserves a full and independent treatment. It is beyond dispute that the work reflects a deep distrust of the jurisdiction administered by the authorities, the *basileis*. There are some references to 'medial judgements', but they cannot be followed up here. The main dangers of jurisdiction by giving an oath to one litigant were that the magistrates might favour one of the litigants by imposing upon him an oath he could swear without any risk (for example by imposing upon Hermes the crooked oath that the cows of Apollo were not in his house), and, secondly, that the litigant might simply commit perjury. Against both these risks the archaic Greek *poleis* took measures.

In Gortyn, as we have seen, the system works on the basis of full trust being placed in the supernatural force of the oath. The only problem was to prevent the magistrates in charge of the jurisdiction indulging in arbitrary acts. This is the political background to the codification of the law in the first half of the fifth century BC. The law code strictly regulates the *dikazein* of the magistrate, as in the example (*IC* IV 72 col. I 17–24) quoted above. If two persons contend about a slave the *dikastas* is ordered to decide that the witness produced by one of the parties has to take the decisive oath. If both parties produce a witness no double oath is allowed: the *dikastas* has himself to give the final decision (*krinein*) on oath. This system presupposes that perjury hardly ever occurs.

About 150 years previously the Athenians had discovered a different solution. From very early on they distrusted oaths sworn by litigants. In every lawsuit each party had to take an oath formulated by the magistrate. Afterwards in special session a jury voted whose oath was the better. These two stages are the basis for Drakon's law of homicide of 621 BC. First we have a *dikazein* by the kings, most probably the *archon basileus* (magistrate) and the leaders of the four *phylai* (clans/tribes), then a *diagignoskein* (resolution) by the fifty-one *ephetai* (court). Wolff assumed that the kings announced the verdict given by the fifty-one *ephetai*; *dikazein* for him was 'the final and authoritative admission of the execution'. Recently (Thür 1987) I have shown that nowhere in ancient Greece did a magistrate announce a verdict given by a jury. I am suspicious also of the assumption that direct control prevails over self-help here. Rather this text fits with those already discussed. Additionally in the fifth and fourth centuries BC in homicide suits each party had to take a solemn oath, called *diomosia* (oath), which was sworn in a preliminary procedure before the *archon basileus*. The name given to this procedure, *prodikasia* (preliminary hearing), reflects *dikazein*. In the main hearing the fifty-one *ephetai* had to decide which of the two oaths was the better. Going back to Drakon, we can assume that in his time also the magistrates imposed the *diomosia* on both litigants—*dikazein*—and afterwards the *ephetai* gave the final decision. There are a few hints that, homicide cases apart, *dikazein*, imposing double oaths by an *archon* (magistrate), and *diagignoskein*, the final decision by a jury, were the most common way of settling legal disputes in archaic Athens (Demosthenes 23. 28; *Lex. Seq.* (Bekker 1965) 242. 19-22, both purporting to date from the time of Solon).

The notion of giving the final decision to a jury of fifty-one citizens, after imposing a double preliminary oath, almost perfectly remedied the abuses complained of by Hesiod. As each party had to swear, neither of the oaths can have been decisive, so no magistrate could favour a single party and perjury does not automatically result in a wrongful judgement. On the other hand an upstanding person would have avoided lawsuits as far as possible so as not to incur the risk of perjury. Again, legal procedure was the last resort. We have seen that the double oaths date from the time before Drakon, so this procedure was not originally connected with democracy. But it led directly to the popular courts of democratic Athens.

Double oaths on the one hand and codification of the law on the other were the first steps taken to break down the divine power of the leaders in the early *poleis*. I do not see an evolution from anarchy to the early Greek state. A more realistic picture is a transition from a sacral to a more secular government. It is amazing to observe how the institutions of legal procedure remained in principle unchanged during this period.[5]

[5] I am grateful to the participants of the seminar I addressed in London for discussion and comments, and especially to the editors of this volume, my colleagues Lin Foxhall and Andrew Lewis, for assistance in the preparation of the final version of this paper.

# 5

## Even Dogs have Erinyes:[1] Sanctions in Athenian Practice and Thinking

### MARGARETHA DEBRUNNER HALL

### 1. INTRODUCTION

In the conclusion of their seminal book on the history of punishment from the Middle Ages to the earlier twentieth century, Rusche and Kirchheimer emphasize: 'The penal system of any given society is not an isolated phenomenon subject to its own special laws. It is an integral part of the whole social system and shares its aspirations and its defects' (1939: 207, cf. 57). A penal system, that is a network of sanctions intended to cover all possible offences which have themselves been clearly defined, did not exist in ancient Greece.[2] Nevertheless, the study of the preoccupations and shortcomings of existing penal regulations is an interesting angle from which to understand the Greek mind. In particular, threats of sanctions can shed light on the values considered worth protecting.

The scanty nature of our evidence only really allows the development of a meaningful general model for Athens, and even there only for the epoch in which court speeches provide us with information additional to the inscriptions on which we are almost completely reliant elsewhere in the Greek world. This paper sets out to ask what late fifth- and fourth-century Athenian practices were when prescribing and enacting sanctions. Whenever possible the results will be compared with material found elsewhere. Two separate questions will be discussed: 1. Did the fact that Athens was a democracy influence the nature and severity of the punishments it imposes? 2. Did the Athenian reputation for mildness (*praotes*)

---

[1] Macarius 3. 54.
[2] For example, what is meant by terms such as *hybris* or *asebeia*? In a decree like that of Kannonous, mentioned by Xenophon (*Hellenika* 1. 7. 20), it is not even clear who should be punished.

which is often remarked upon (Lysias 6. 34; Aristotle, *Constitution of the Athenians* 22. 4; Demosthenes 19. 104; 58. 55) affect their administration of justice?[3]

I shall concentrate mainly on the forms of punishment Athens prescribed and applied, and leave aside some related but relevant questions concerning penal law: the evidence will not permit us to maintain a clear distinction between laws which merely prescribe sanctions and the reality of force.[4] A modern mind might too easily take it for granted that a sanction laid down in law would be enforced and that punishment would only be meted out if there was a law prescribing it. In Athens, however, the principle 'no penalty without a law' in its strict form was not maintained, and it was conceivably possible to punish someone for a 'wrong' which no law had defined as such. This peculiarity has to be seen against the background that the Athenians in general were much less concerned with defining offences than they were with procedure, a fact long recognized but deserving emphasis (Todd and Millett 1990: 5, quoting Sir Henry Maine in 1883). An attempt therefore to distinguish mere prescription from force in Athens would not only considerably reduce the basis for any model, it would also distort the picture.

In principle there were three ways a penalty could be determined in an individual case. For some offences the law permitted immediate seizure and summary execution, either prescribing these sanctions through magistrates or by endorsing self-help. In classical Athens I believe this hardly ever happened. Once a case was brought to a regular court there existed two types of verdict. In the first type, the 'unassessed case' (*agon* or *dike atimetos*), the law contained a mandatory penalty for those convicted. In the second type, the 'assessed case' (*timetos*), after a condemnation the court had to hold a second vote to choose between the proposals for a suitable punishment suggested by both parties (Lipsius 1905-15: 248-52;

---

[3] The frequency with which Demosthenes has to argue that sometimes this mildness does harm (for example, it works for the wrongdoers in 21. 184; it is all right in private laws but not in public ones, 24. 69, 192 f.; it encourages other criminals, 24. 218, 51. 12) indicates that in general the Athenians prided themselves on it as part of their democratic life-style (cf. Demosthenes 24. 69).

[4] To take a modern example, arson in Her Majesty's dockyard was punishable by death in British law until quite recently. But since in the last few decades nobody had been found guilty of this particular offence most people would have said that Britain had abolished the death penalty.

cf. Plato, *Apology* 36–38b). I do not attempt a systematic discussion of the relationship between these three ways of fixing a penalty.

A third area to which I can only make passing reference is the relationship between the nature and gravity of the offence and the punishment meted out for it. A study of this problem would have to give special consideration to this society's reaction to homicide and its complex development. But Cohen (1983a) is right in saying that the relatively rare incidence of culpable homicide has up to now attracted a disproportionate amount of interest, to the detriment of 'other areas which would be more useful in exploring the Athenian conception of crime, criminality and public offenders' (Cohen 1983a: 1 n. 3). In accordance with the theoretical guidelines suggested by Cohen, I will analyse forms of punishment in terms of how they fit the Athenian image of their own democratic behaviour and the mildness of which they were so proud.

## 2. THE RANGE OF ATHENIAN PENALTIES

### 2.1. Fines

Probably the most common form of punishment in classical Athens was the imposition of fines, varying proportions of which went to the injured party, the public purse, or informers, depending on the offence (MacDowell 1978: 257 ff.; cf. Gernet 1936 1981b: 247). Many fines were the consequence of not fulfilling a contractual obligation such as finishing a building by a certain date, or the non-payment of debts (e.g. Demosthenes 56. 27, 38; 53. 10; see also Lipsius 1905–15: 688 ff., and outside Athens, 689 n. 42). Such cases often must have been resolved out of court, either by: (1) seizure of securities by the creditor (Isaios 5. 22-4, MacDowell 1978: 153), or (2) with the help of minor magistrates such as the *astynomoi* (Harrison 1971: 25), or (3) one of the official or unofficial arbitrators in Athens (Aristotle *Constitution of the Athenians* 53. 4-6; see also Demosthenes 21. 92, 33. 31-3), whose activities are only rarely mentioned in the sources though they might have been quite extensive.

A whole network of regulated payments to the courts protected them from being unnecessarily burdened with private financial quarrels: for example some cases were only dealt with after both sides had paid a deposit fixed according to the value of the disputed sum. The loser would then have to pay the deposit for both

(Demosthenes 47. 64; Harpocration, s.v. *prytaneia*; Harrison 1971: 179–83; cf. Böckh 1886: 415–39; Lipsius 1905–15: 824–8). This amounted to a fine for misusing the courts. Likewise in most public cases, all of which depended on someone volunteering to prosecute (the *boulomenos*), the accuser could expect as a reward part of the fine extracted from the person convicted if his suit were successful, but he also risked a fine of 1,000 drachmai and *atimia* (disenfranchisement, see below, Sect. 2.3) should he convince less than one-fifth of the jurors that the accused was indeed guilty.

The sources give us a little more information about the cases decided by courts, and occasionally also tell us which offences were fined and how heavily (for examples see Böckh 1886: 439–54). The spectrum is very wide and too scanty to allow a systematic and statistically meaningful study of patterns. The following examples can nevertheless show the kind of information provided by laws prescribing fines.

In an action for abusive language (*dike kakegorias*) the plaintiff could make his adversary pay 500 drachmae, of which 200 were claimed by the city (Lex. Cantabr., s.v. *kakegorias dike*, see Lipsius 1905–15: 646–51). In light of the mutual mud-slinging normally found in court speeches it is perhaps surprising how few such cases are attested. Were they often settled by arbitrators, as in Demosthenes 21. 32? Was the law allowing such an action just a feeble attempt to limit excesses?

The unauthorized removal of sacred olive trees from a sanctuary led to a fine of 200 drachmae, half for the city and half for the informer (Demosthenes 43. 71). Like many other laws, this one provides what seems to be a generous incentive for volunteers who bring offences against the state's interest to public notice: half the fine.

Intentional material harm (*blabe*) was punished by imposing a fine of double the value of the actual damage, as opposed to non-intentional damage where restitution only was granted (Lipsius 1905–15: 652–63). This reflects, as Demosthenes said (21. 43), the principle that the intention of the offender matters for the question of how severe a punishment he deserves. The significance of intentionality for guilt in homicide cases has long been recognized (R. Loening 1903; Maschke 1926). It need only be noted here that it also had implications for relatively minor matters such as material damage.

The violation of a free woman, according to Plutarch (*Life of Solon* 23. 1), was punished by a fine of only 100 drachmai, of which half was paid into the public treasury.[5] Lysias (1. 32) says the punishment was only 'double the damage' for the rapist (as in the case of intentional material damage), whilst the seducer (*moikhos*) had to face the death penalty, since the lawgiver believed that the seducer had corrupted the soul of the woman. Although this passage is problematic and its interpretation is controversial, if the Athenians indeed punished rape with a fine and considered it a form of 'damage', it indicates the weak position of women within Athenian law.[6]

A demarch who neglected to bury the body of a foreigner found in his deme was liable to a fine of 1,000 drachmae. Compared with the examples mentioned so far this is a large sum. The same fine, though, was prescribed for a *choregos* who smuggled a foreign dancer into his chorus at the theatre of Dionysos (Plutarch, *Phokion* 30), and for an archon in charge of weights and measures who neglected his duties (in a law from about 100 BC, *IG* II² 1013). Each member of the *boule* who failed to exact money for the lease of the land of the temple of Kodros, Neleus, and Basile was to have been fined 1,000 drachmai. The archon who failed to do his duty in the same context faced a fine of 10,000 drachmai (Sokolowski 1969: no. 14 = *IG* I³ 81, from 418/7 BC). This very high sum makes one doubt that this fine was ever imposed: its inclusion in the law might merely mean that the legislator wanted to convey that this was a serious issue. One might even go further and say that the threat of such a large fine is in effect an expression of powerlessness, of hope that the law would act as a deterrent rather than an expectation that sanctions could be imposed if flouted.

Or does this evidence suggest that in general abuse and neglect of official duties were punished more severely or at least considered more serious than offences by private individuals in Athens? If so this would tally well with a central feature of democracy, namely

---

[5] An attempt to compare this sum with those for the same offence in the famous laws of Gortyn *IC* IV 72 col. II 2 ff. is impossible. How are we to compare 100 staters in Gortyn with 100 drachmai in Athens (if we can believe Plutarch's figure at all)? It is noteworthy that in Gortyn the law does not distinguish the rape of a man from that of a woman; the penalty is the same.

[6] On the problems of interpretation of the Lysias passage and the distinctions between rape and adultery see Cohen (1991, 1983b;) E. Harris (1990); Cantarella (1991); Foxhall (1991).

the rigorous accountability of all officials to the *demos*, the people (de Ste Croix 1981: 285; Aristotle, *Politics* 1282ᵇ26; Herodotos 3. 80). In the absence of public prosecutors elsewhere in Athens it is remarkable that only here, for the control of officials, do we find regular procedures which in practice functioned as a form of institutionalized prosecution. Once each prytany, an *apocheirotonia* (a vote against any office-holder, amounting to a vote of no confidence) could depose any of the 700 or so officials immediately. A deposed official could then be accused under a procedure such as that of *eisangelia* (perhaps best viewed as a kind of impeachment), and was liable to be punished by anything from a fine to exile and death. At the end of the year each of the officials had to undergo an audit of his conduct, the *euthynai*. Should any irregularities come to light the procedure would have automatically led to a trial against him. These regulations were more than a preventive means to guarantee proper conduct in office. Generals especially were often tried and condemned to heavy fines or worse (for example, Timotheos, Isocrates 15. 129). Demosthenes (4. 47), who claimed that in Athens for a general the risk of being sentenced to death was greater than the risk of being killed in battle, was not far from the mark (Hansen 1975: 59–64; J. Roberts 1982).

The most extreme form of fine, the confiscation of an individual's entire fortune, is often just an addition to the more severe punishments of death or *atimia*, but can occasionally occur on its own (Harrison 1971: 178 f.; Lipsius 1905–15: 595 n. 18).[7] In practice there must have been a big difference between imposing a mere fine and confiscation of everything. After a fine one's reputation was somewhat damaged but otherwise one could continue to live as a citizen among fellow citizens. But taking everything from a person was, in actuality, excluding him from his life as he lived it up to then.

## 2.2  Imprisonment, detention, and corporal punishment

The other common form of punishment today, imprisonment, was very rare in Athens and some scholars have doubted whether it was ever a punishment as opposed to mere detention until a case was tried or a debt paid (Lipsius 1905–15: 932; Harrison 1971:

---

[7]  It is right, though, to doubt the interpretation of Demosthenes 20. 40 as implying full loss of fortune for refusal to take on a liturgy.

177; MacDowell 1978: 257; Ruschenbusch 1968: 13, 27-47).[8]
An interpretation of this fact without a careful study of the 'pre-
history of punishment' (to use Cantarella's 1984 title), especially
the emergence of some kind of police to guard prisoners, must
remain incomplete. However, in comparison with penal institutions
which have used their prisoners as productive labour, as the
Romans sometimes did,[9] it might be noted that the idea of using
convicts as labour seems not to have occurred to the Athenians.
(This does not need an explanation. What does need an explanation, as Foucault 1977 and others have shown, is why this practice has occurred in modern times.)

Two passages seem to attest the existence of some sort of stock
as an additional punishment for some thieves, but otherwise punishments which primarily dishonoured the punished, such as the
pillory, are not documented for ancient Athens (cf. Latte 1968a:
310). Equally noteworthy is the absence of corporal punishment
and torture for citizens. Only the whipping of slaves, for offences for
which free men paid fines, is known. For example, *IG* II² 1362 (=
Sokolowski 1969: no. 37), a late-fourth-century law protecting the
trees around the sanctuary of Apollo Erithaseus, provided a fifty
drachma fine for free trespassers and fifty strokes with the lash for
slaves. Unfortunately the evidence does not allow us to see whether
the Athenians in this regard were different from other Greek
cities.

### 2.3 *Atimia* ('Disenfranchisement')

The term *atimia* covered a further wide spectrum of Athenian forms
of punishment (Hansen 1976: 55-90). It is the 'total or partial loss
of rights' and by definition 'as a penalty only pertinent to citizens'
(ibid.56). *Atimia* could either be automatically imposed if a law provided immediate imposition (as for example disobeying the call-up
for military service, Demosthenes 24. 103-5), or it could be
inflicted by sentence of a court. Sometimes *atimia* was temporary:
state debtors immediately regained full citizen status upon payment
of their debt, or, on the other hand, their debt along with the *atimia*

---

[8] For the wider Greek context see Latte (1968a: 295).
[9] For the Roman use of convict labour, see, *Digest* 48. 19. 28. 6 (Hadrianic). On
the context see Burdon 1988. The closest to a long-term sentence as working prisoners occurred in the quarries of Syracuse (Latte 1968a: 295), though the source
(Aelian, *VH* 12. 44) does not explicitly say that these men and women worked.

could be inherited by their sons. Permanent *atimia*, sometimes even extending to the whole family, could be imposed on traitors or people who had proposed the abolition of certain laws (Hansen 1976: 71). A connection between all offences punished with *atimia* is impossible, but Hansen (ibid.72) shows that they seem to be mainly 'for not complying with an injunction rather than for defying a prohibition'. These delicts were in the largest sense neglect of civil duties, though not offences against property or acts of violence (ibid.72–4 lists offences punished by *atimia*, with the supporting evidence). With the threat and imposition of *atimia* the Athenians could in theory make sure that the citizens did indeed perform their duties. The efficiency of these provisions depended though on the enforceability of the punishment, a problem to which I shall return in Section 3.

## 2.4 The death penalty

The gravest penalty the Athenians could impose was of course death. Information about actual executions is scarce and difficult to interpret (Latte 1968: 393–415). Many studies taking a historical-anthropological perspective have tried to account for different means of communal killing attested in the Greek world (Gernet 1981b; Loraux 1984; Gras 1984; Cantarella 1987, 1988; Berneker 1971; Whitehorne 1989). One aspect of the thorny question when, how, and for which offences the community imposed and enforced the death penalty is discussed with exemplary clarity by Thür (1988). For my question, whether the Athenians were particularly mild, humane, and democratic in their penal laws, I can leave aside these problems and ask how did Athenians in the later fifth and fourth centuries BC normally kill offenders? Everybody knows that Sokrates was given hemlock. Letting him thus commit suicide was an exceptional privilege[10] in what may have been a

---

[10] Allusions which show that the poison and its effect were well known (Aristophanes, *Frogs* 124, 1051, cf. Plato, *Lysias* 219e) are no proof that it was a penalty administered by the state. The only attested executions by hemlock are those of Sokrates and Theramenes (Xenophon, *Hellenika* 2. 3. 56). Both are cases of prominent men in exceptional political circumstances. Andokides 3. 10 is probably also an allusion to Theramenes, and perhaps to a few other victims of the Thirty. There is no evidence to support the view of Bonner and Smith (1938: 285) that hemlock was introduced by the Thirty as the normal form of death penalty. The 'expert' who brought Sokrates the cup (Plato, *Phaedo* 117a) remains a problem. In Rome the

very exceptional situation in any case: even in homicide trials[11] the accused had the option to go into voluntary exile unharmed after the first of the two speeches allowed to the defence (Demosthenes 21. 43; 23. 45; 23. 69 f., but excepting parricides: Antiphon 5. 13; Pollux 8. 117, Lipsius 1905-15: 811). It seems a plausible assumption, therefore, that anyone awaiting a trial and expecting a death penalty who had the means to establish an existence outside Athens will have preferred exile. In other words, the actual execution of even only moderately wealthy citizens condemned to death by a court must have been very rare. Is this an indication of particular mildness on the part of the Athenians or of the weakness of Athens? I think neither, but before I can defend my view a few words on summary execution are necessary.

The laws on *kakourgoi* ('evil-doers') covered in particular thieves and burglars (Kränzlein 1963: 138-43; Hansen 1976; Cohen 1983a: 52-61). These when caught red-handed could be brought before the Eleven and were executed right away. They were given a court hearing only if they denied committing the crime of which they were accused. If the court then found them guilty after all they were killed without the option of going into exile. How often such executions really took place can only be guessed. Cohen (1983a: 8) thinks that probably the majority of thieves were dealt with by a summary procedure before the Eleven. Even allowing for the fact that such offences as theft and burglary were probably relatively petty felonies of which only the minority of cases was ever brought to justice in court (rather than being settled out of court in other ways), it seems likely that such executions were the most frequently administered form of death penalty in ancient Athens. Who were the convicted? The large majority of them must have come from the lower social classes (Hansen 1976: 121) or were even foreigners, non-citizens, or slaves. Hence they had fewer means to defend their lives. Even if they got a court hearing as opposed to a mere hue and cry procedure, they could not afford to employ a Lysias or an Antiphon (Cohen 1983: 7). In light of this the suspicions of the rich, that the popular courts were biased against them,

choice between suicide or exile seems clearly to have been a privilege for people from the upper classes (Kunkel 1962: 67-78). For the interpretation of hemlock as 'permitted but controlled suicide' see Gernet (1981a: 255. Further discussions of the problem can be found in Bonner 1973.

[11] Except for parricides (Pollux 8.117), which must have been unusual in Athens; I know of no attested examples.

appear in a different light. The wealthy at least had the opportunity of ready access to the courts. Athenians exercised to some extent a class justice.

The image of Athens' mildness receives an even more severe blow when we ask how these petty offenders died. The method employed was not straightforward hanging or beheading but a form of crucifixion, the *apotympanismos*.[12] After being fixed naked onto poles with iron clamps around their necks, wrists, and ankles (like Aeschylus' Prometheus in *Prometheus Bound* on his rock, see Cantarella 1984: 52-9), the victims were left in the open air (where exactly we do not know) to die from thirst and exhaustion. This could take several days, since unlike crucified men who had pierced hands and feet, these men attached to poles did not lose blood (Gernet [1924] 1981: 254). How quickly death came about also depended on whether the poles were upright (see Ducrey 1971). I do not enter the discussion of when and how the Athenians began this practice,[13] but wish to emphasize that this slow and cruel method of execution was the normal way of punishing *kakourgoi* at the period with which I am concerned.[14]

Why then *apotympanismos*? Was it for religious reasons, to avoid the shedding of blood and the ensuing pollution? Then hanging and strangulation might have done.[15] Was the idea that by exposing the body to nature (heat, thirst, hunger, wild animals) the community was merely ensuring that death would ensue rather than actively bringing it about (Thür 1988: 148)? But then this could have been done this less publicly, as Kreon locked Antigone up in her tomb.

---

[12] For the wider context of crucifixion see Hengel (1977: 70 ff.), and generally on *apotympanismos*.

[13] Gernet 1981a: 52-76) discussed at length the implications of Kermapoullos's 1923 archaeological discovery of a mass grave at Phaleron of the 7th century BC containing the skeletons of 17 people who had died by *apotympanismos*, with the clamps still on their bodies. Thür (1988: 148 f.) is certainly right in doubting an interpretation of this find as the result of a death penalty for murder, and he refers to further literature on the problem (ibid. n. 24).

[14] Known cases of *apotympanismos* with their number in brackets in Hansen's catalogue (1976: 122-43): Lysias 13. 67 f. (6); 13. 55-7 (11). Execution attested, method not specified but *apotympanismos* possible: Lysias 13. 1-4, 39-42, 82-97 (12). *Apotympanismos* mentioned: Demosthenes 8. 61; 19. 137; Aristotle, *Rhetoric* 2. 1383$^a$5.

[15] Though Loraux (1984) argues that strangulation, whether imposed or as suicide, was seen as a particularly female way to die and was considered particularly shameful.

One cannot escape the impression that the slow, painful, and public nature of death was deliberate and was also intended to humiliate (see also Gernet's interpretation, 1981a: 264; 1981b: 243, of the pillory as a milder form of *apotympanismos*). The way it was used as a punishment appears to be a very strong statement about how importantly private property was valued, and by implication the significance of the integrity of the *oikos* (household) for the Athenians. Another piece of evidence shows clearly that a high priority was given to protecting private property: the first thing the new eponymous archon did in Athens was to announce that whatever anybody owned before he, the speaker, took office, the owner would keep until the end of his year as archon (Aristotle, *Constitution of the Athenians* 56.2, see also Jones 1956: 198, 207).

The death penalty could be made particularly severe by denying burial in Attika afterwards, though this was, I believe, a very rare occurrence and possibly limited to the most serious political crimes. (I follow Whitehorne 1989 in disputing that to throw somebody into the *barathron* (pit) was to deny him burial.) At least two of the leading members of the coup of 411 BC, Archeptolemos and Antiphon, were executed by the Eleven. They and their families were declared *atimoi* and the family fortune was confiscated by the state. In addition to this they were denied burial in Athenian territory ([Plutarch], *Lives of the Ten Orators* 834a and b). Another oligarch, Phrynichos, was tried posthumously and his bones dug up and removed from Attica (Lykourgos, *Against Leokrates* 113). His murderers received public honours (Meiggs and Lewis 1988: no. 85).

## 2.5 *Athenian punishment: a summary*

With my survey of the main Athenian forms of punishment complete, I can now give preliminary answers to my original questions, though new questions are raised. (1) If indeed officials were punished more severely than others, this should be linked with the democratic principle of official accountability, and the penal regulations do thus reflect Athenian political principles. But to defend such a view one would have to show that in this regard Athens differed from other Greek cities. (2) The virtual absence in Athens of corporal punishment, and the use of penalties whose main aim was to disgrace without severe injury, seems to be a sure sign of a fairly humane society. But again, was Athens here exceptional? (3) Was *atimia*, the partial exclusion or expulsion of those who failed to conform with the legal expectations of civic life, a sign of Athens' mildness? Did it exist elsewhere? Certainly *apotympanismos*, the harsh form of death penalty for *kakourgoi*, and possibly also for *atimoi*, seems offensive and barbaric to modern eyes. It is hard to reconcile with our idea of a society priding itself on its mildness.

### 3. PUNISHMENT IN OTHER GREEK CITIES IN COMPARISON WITH ATHENS

Sokolowski's three volumes of '*lois sacrées*' (1955, 1963, 1969) provide a useful starting-point for approaching the question of whether particularly heavy fines or other penalties for officials were a specifically 'democratic' feature of Athenian law. The editor does not explicitly define the criteria which make a text a *loi sacrée*. His collected inscriptions are all loosely linked with regulating cult practices. They are not concerned with metaphysics or beliefs. They provide a handy selection of geographically and chronologically (sixth century BC to second century AD) widely spread examples.

Among the sanctions prescribed the large majority are fines or related forms of material loss, such as losing an animal to the temple which has been allowed to graze without permission on temple land (Sokolowski 1969: no. 79), or having to dedicate to the goddess the excessively luxurious dress worn for the cult festival (1969: no. 68; 1963: no. 32). A substantial number of these fines were prescribed for officials who neglected their duty, especially that of maintaining the laws and collecting fines from trespassers (1955: nos. 33, 52, 53, 70; 1963: nos. 24, 32, 44, 121; 1969: nos. 66, 83, 91, 93, 115, 122, 144, 173; and from Athens, 1969: nos. 3, 5, 14; 1963: no. 12). Punishments for not taking steps against culprits can be the same or even higher than those for the primary offender.[16] Some of these laws even regulate which body was to supervise and punish the magistrate who was in charge of initiating procedures and had to impose sanctions. For example, a fourth-century law from Euboea protecting a sacred grove threat-

---

[16] Fine the same for primary offender and official responsible for enforcing the law: Sokolowski (1969): nos. 66, 115, 144. Fine doubled for the enforcing official: Meiggs and Lewis (1988): no. 2; Buck (1955): no. 61; Sokolowski (1969): no. 91. Relationship between fine for offender and fine for official unclear: Buck (1955): nos. 16, 61; Sokolowski (1963): nos. 3, 12, 24.

ened trespassers with a fine of 50 drachmai, while the demarch who did not make sure this fine was paid or an oath of innocence sworn was punished with a fine of 500 drachmai, and the *hieropoioi* who failed to exact payment of fines were liable to double the sums (Sokolowski 1969: no. 91; compare also Buck 1955: no. 61, from Elis before 580 BC). It therefore becomes evident that strict laws and punishments for officials were not limited to Athens, and democratic accountability does not sufficiently explain the phenomenon.

A convincing interpretation would have to set these laws in the context of what was probably the central problem of penal law in Greek city-states, namely enforcement. After the first hurdle in bringing a culprit to justice, which was to ensure that someone brought the case to the notice of the relevant official, the community had to make sure that the official did indeed properly initiate procedures. This was not as straightforward a matter as it might seem. If the accused person was an influential man or a personal friend of the official or just offered a bribe, the temptation simply not to get the legal procedures started might sometimes have been quite strong, hence the necessity to threaten heavy fines for yielding to this temptation. The severity of these fines expressed how important the community thought it was that their officials behaved justly. There must have been a real worry that they might abuse their position (Humphreys 1983), not so much in doing wrong as in not doing their duty and thereby blocking the course of justice, causing social tensions, and endangering the possessions and lives of the citizens. The fact that laws containing threats against officials occur at all, and continue to crop up in many places right through the Classical and Hellenistic periods (for example Buck 1955: no. 120.29 lines ff., Dreros third to second century BC) reveals that there was a perceived need for these laws based on a strong awareness of how much a community depends on keepers of order fulfilling their duties.

Corporal punishment for free men seems to have been absent from the Greek world (Latte 1968a: 295). Athens was not a laudable exception here. Whipping slaves instead of fining them is also attested elsewhere besides Athens (Sokolowski 1969: nos. 37, 53, 84, 125, 149; Klaffenbach 1954: col. IV 184–96). Apart from being an expression of inferior social status this distinction probably had a practical reason: it was the only way to punish slaves.[17]

[17] The punishing of slaves could also be seen as a way of educating them, Aristotle, *Rhetoric* 2, 1380$^a$17. Cf. Debrunner (1988: 680 f.)

Their death would have been a material loss for the owner, *atimia* would have been pointless, and only a small minority would have had any money to pay a fine.

For *atimia* in the sense of exile, parallels can be found from outside Athens (Latte 1968a: 297). In light of the limited evidence it is more difficult to find out whether the concept of *atimia* could have so many facets elsewhere as it had in Athens. It is also hard to know how frequently it was administered elsewhere. In Amphipolis in 357 BC we find 'eternal exile' (*aeiphygia*) (Buck 1955: no.12 = Tod 1948: no. 150). Does this imply that there was temporary exile as well in the local laws? A Lokrian law of the early fifth century imposed *atimia* for non-payment of taxes (Buck 1955: no. 57, lines 14 ff.), and the same text threatened magistrates who did not do their duty in bringing criminals to justice with *atimia* and confiscation of property. Thus even a superficial glance at texts from elsewhere reveals similar features to those found in Athens. An Athenian might have argued that *atimia* was the most Athenian form of punishment. It is hard enough to be exiled from anywhere, but losing the rights and privileges of Athenian citizenship is particularly disadvantageous. Not only does an Athenian citizen have more rights to exercise in participating in public life, but also Athens' sphere of influence is very wide and the options for a life away from Athens are therefore especially limited. Citizen rights are particularly good in a democracy and the threat of losing them is an effective way of making people actively maintain the laws. Whether these sorts of claims would have been justified is hard to know, because comparable evidence for civic pride in other cities is lacking.

Finally let us turn to the drastic death penalty of *apotympanismos*. It is difficult to find texts anywhere in Greece which specify the way convicted men and women were actually killed.[18] As Loraux (1984: 195) shows, this might be explained with a general 'Greek tendency to euphemize death in all its forms' (see also Hengel 1977: 69–83). It seems, however, that *apotympanismos* is once

[18] A search for non-Athenian laws on stone prescribing the death penalty in Tod (1948); Meiggs and Lewis (1988); Sokolowski (1955, 1963, 1969), and Buck (1955) yielded one single instance: a late fifth-early-fourth-century law from Mytilene (Buck 1955: no. 25 = Tod 1948: no. 112), the famous coinage agreement with Phocaea in which it is prescribed that an official who was found to have intentionally debased the metal value of the coins should be executed. On the death penalty in Greece in general see Latte (1968b).

attested outside Athens, in this case for a slave who killed his master and burnt the house (Latte 1968b: 400; Robert and Robert 1983: 261-3). The date, second to first century BC, suggests Roman influence (Hengel 1977: 76). Even without comparative evidence which might have shown other Greek cities to have even nastier forms of execution, and even if it could be proved that the death penalty in Athens was applied much less often than elsewhere, Athens was not as mild and humane as the Athenians generally liked to perceive their city to be. This fact has obviously worried Bonner and Smith (1938), whose seminal book conveys a general picture of a humane Athens. In an attempt to salvage this image they wrote:

This harsh and inhumane law was part of an ancient legislation which, for general traditional reasons in later times, the Athenians preserved with reverence and firmness as a shield of their democratic organization. It *seems preferable*, however, to regard death as brought about by strangulation, rather than by bloodless crucifixion. (Bonner and Smith 1938: 281, emphasis mine)

Bonner and Smith then quote three texts to support this view. The first, Aristophanes' *Thesmophoriazousai* 1053 f., describes how Mnesilochos is tied onto a board by a Scythian archer and how he laments. This might indeed be a parody of an *apotympanismos* (Gernet 1981a: 260 agrees, Latte 1968b: 401 f. and Colin Austin (pers. comm.) are doubtful). Mnesilochos complains in particular of 'throat-cutting pain' (λαιμότμητ' ἄχη, *laimotmet' ache*), and says that he is on the way to Hades on 'fiery sticks' (αἰόλα πυρεία, *aiola pyreia*). The adjective *aiolos* is taken by Bonner and Smith to mean 'quick', and hence they take the passage to express the speed of death by *apotympanismos*. This is possible, but *aiolos* could equally well mean 'slippery', and in any case the text of the passage seems to be corrupt. This alone would not be a sound basis for a whole theory of Athenian penal practice.

The second passage (Aristotle *Rhetoric* 2.1385ᵃ10 ff.) is no more helpful in supporting the view that *apotympanismos* involved humanely quick strangulation. The episode takes place in Syracuse, where the poet Antiphon is about to be executed by the tyrant of the city Dionysios. One of his fellow convicts hides his face, and Antiphon ask him, 'why do you hide what tomorrow everybody will see?' This does not prove that the man will be dead, only that he will not be able any longer to hide his face.

The third passage is a comment of Plutarch's (*Life of Perikles* 28. 2 f.) on Perikles' behaviour in Samos in 439 BC. Samian officers were fastened onto planks and exposed to the public for ten days, then their skulls were crushed. Plutarch doubted this report by Douris of Samos: it was, he said, invented to discredit the Athenians. Bonner and Smith (1938) argued that had *apotympanismos* without strangulation been the normal death penalty, this treatment of the Samians would not have been noteworthy. But they fail to consider the rest of the passage in Plutarch: Perikles forbade the Samians to bury the men who had thus died. It is this which makes the execution exceptionally cruel, not the long exposure (Gernet 1981a: 267, who argued that some kind of burial after *apotympanismos* was normal). In short, the desperate attempt of Bonner and Smith (1938), which has been implicitly and explicitly followed by many other scholars, to salvage the image of a humane Athens clearly fails.

### 4. CONCLUSIONS

I have argued that the Athenians did not differ significantly from their fellow Greeks in other cities in the ways they punished or threatened malefactors. In this area their claim to be especially mild and particularly democratic cannot be maintained (for a particularly dark view of the Athenian administration of justice see Hansen 1976: 119–21).

However, two features of Athenian penal practice made the city unusual among Greek cities in the eyes of modern observers. First, Athens seems to show a particularly intense preoccupation with procedure. One could argue that the provision of a range of procedures to get redress allowed access to the courts (and in principle to justice) openly to all citizens alike and was thus more democratic (Osborne 1985). Second, there is the apparently unique institution of the mass courts and the elaborate procedures to prevent them from being corrupted (Aristotle, *Constitution of the Athenians* 63. 4 ff.). To have so many judges will have reduced the danger that individual prejudice or bribery influenced the administration of justice. Indeed, the accused who was able to plead his case well may have stood a better chance of being acquitted. This could be understood as courts with a milder disposition. So if there is a claim for Athens to be different, more democratic, and milder in its criminal justice, it could only be justified by referring to the modes of procedure, not the nature and severity of the forms of punishment.

A further factor marked Athens out from other cities. Here, mainly in the court speeches of the fourth century BC, we find the earliest explicit comments on the nature of punishment, reflections on its function as satisfying the psychological need for revenge, restoring justice, as a deterrent, and thereby protecting the contemporary order (for example, Aischines 1. 34, 36, 113, 186 ff., 3.8; Demosthenes 21. 7 f., 30, 34). These are, in fact, the main tenets of all later penal theory. But it might be just the distribution of our evidence, coming mainly from Athens, which conveys the impression that only there did people begin to reflect on the philosophical problems of punishment. It seems more likely that these ideas emerged from the sophistic movement, and indeed the first major theorist of penology was probably Protagoras, who influenced not only Plato and Athenian thinking in general, but also people all over the Greek world (Plato, *Protagoras* 323c–324d; also Mackenzie 1981; Saunders 1981 and this volume). We simply do not have court speeches from, for example Syracuse. If any had survived they might have contained instructive incidental remarks on penology too.

In conclusion, the Athenians did not differ from other Greek cities in their choice of punishment, their severity, and their thinking about the fundamental ethical problems of punishing (Debrunner 1988: 685, 692–4). Neither can their claim to a milder or more humane administration of justice be substantiated by a study of their penal practices. The mildness upon which Athenians prided themselves should not lead modern historians to confuse democratic laws and political structure with particularly humane behaviour. Athens was in many ways unique but it was nevertheless also an ancient Greek *polis*, no better nor worse than any of its neighbours.

# 6

## Plato on the Treatment of Heretics[1]

### TREVOR J. SAUNDERS

#### 1. PLATONIC PENOLOGY

Before embarking on this summary the reader needs to be made aware of the key features of Platonic penology. In his *Laws* and elsewhere Plato argues, in a radically utilitarian spirit, that punishment ought not to be inflicted with an eye to the past, retributively and vindictively, but solely with a view to the future: it should be so calculated as to 'cure' the offender, not merely by brute deterrence, but by affecting his mental state and moral outlook for the better. But efficient 'cure' demands efficient diagnosis; and at many points in the model penal code he describes in the *Laws* Plato therefore pays close attention to the analysis of many different criminal states of mind. The chapter here summarized is a study of how in pursuit of this reformative policy he adopted and adapted the Athenian legislation on 'impiety' (*asebeia*); we observe a philosopher working creatively on the raw material of contemporary law.

#### 2. ATHENIAN AND PLATONIC IMPIETY

On a strict view, it is not possible to compare the Platonic law of impiety with the Athenian. The gods of Greek popular belief were human beings writ large: immortal and more powerful than we, sometimes benevolent and sometimes malign, with an unstable devotion to moral virtue. The bulk of the Athenian law of impiety therefore concerned a wide variety of acts supposed to be likely to attract the gods' hostility: (i) infractions of ritual, (ii) insulting language or behaviour to themselves or their property or images,

[1] This is a summary of a paper originally delivered as one of the series collected in this volume. An expanded and more deatiled version of the argument presented here was subsequently published as a chapter in Saunders 1991: 301-23. For further evidence and argumentation the reader is invited to turn to that book.

(iii) revealing the 'mysteries' of certain cults, (iv) entering holy places when in a state of *atimia* ('disfranchisement'), and (v) introducing new or foreign divinities. When (vi) it forbade the advancing of *opinions* about the gods, notably atheism and certain doctrines about the physical nature of the heavenly bodies, it was to protect the popular view of gods as personal beings able to harm men or benefit them, especially by ignoring or condoning offences, in return for sacrifices and prayers.

Plato's gods are by contrast wholly incorruptible. They are always benevolent to us; divine punishment is intended, as legal punishment ought to be, to make us morally better, and therefore, in the Sokratic/Platonic view, happier. The wise man ought therefore to strive to imitate the gods, and make his own character like theirs. Plato accordingly concentrates on a set of beliefs and practices which tend to rob the gods of their role as protectors of moral virtue. His law has very little to say about (i)–(v) above; but its provisions for (vi), heretical opinion, are of enormous length and elaboration.

### 3. THE ATHENIAN LAW

At least some of the prosecutions of Sokrates and other intellectuals for impiety seem to have taken place under the 'decree of Diopeithes', which probably dates from the 430s and may have been recast later in the century as a regular *graphe asebeias*, suit for impiety (Cohen 1991: 203–17). According to Plutarch (*Life of Perikles* 32. 1), the decree provided, vaguely enough, that 'those who do not recognize the divine things, or who teach doctrines about the things in the sky', should be impeached (*eisangellesthai*). To judge from the accounts of the individual cases, the penalty was assessed by the court; instances of fines, exile, and death are reported. Plato's law against impiety thus has solid Athenian antecedents; for he too wishes to suppress expressions of atheism and merely mechanical explanations of the workings of the heavens.

### 4. THE PLATONIC 'HERESY' LAW

In book 10 of the *Laws* Plato identifies three heresies: (i) atheism; (ii) the gods' indifference to the human race; (iii) their willingness to be won over by prayer and sacrifice (*Laws* 885b; all subsequent references to Plato are to the *Laws*). His law, like Diopeithes' decree, is directed not against the mere holding of heretical opinions in one's own mind, or even against their casual expression, but against their propagation. It has two chief features (907d until the end of the book).[2] (1) It is cast in terms of damage. The heretic who persuades a man that the gods do not punish vice, because they can be deflected by bribes in the shape of sacrifices or supplications, encourages him in immorality, and therefore diminishes his happiness, his self-fulfilment as a human being. Heresy therefore, if propagated, inflicts harm. (2) What then becomes important in assessing a heretic's punishment is less his heresy itself, than his character, demeanour, intellect, and his mastery of the arts of persuasion.

Plato accordingly distinguishes two categories of heretics. The first is naturally just, lives uprightly, and hates scoundrels; he is humorous, frank, and ultimately foolish; but if he is not punished, he will make converts. The second, described by Plato at passionate length, lacks control over his pleasures and pains; he is powerful intellectually, and is full of guile. He is beast-like, and despise and bewitches his hearers, by promising to bewitch the dead and persuade the gods by recourse to sacrifices and charms. He tries to wreck individuals, whole houses, and indeed states, for the sake of money. Such heretics typically become magicians, tyrants, popular orators, generals, and plotters in private rites.

Plato's law is rich in penological interest, and can be analyzed as presenting ten problems, not all of them soluble.

### 4.1 Problem 1: opinion and action

Plato's diffuse exposition makes it hard to establish how far a distinction between (i) holding and propagating heresy, and (ii) acting on it, is functional in the law. On close examination, the text provides penalties for heresy-inspired actions entirely separately from those for propagation of opinion. The heresy law proper concerns only the latter; and it focuses on the character, belief, and reformability of the offenders.

### 4.2 Problem 2: six or two categories of heretics (908b ff.)?

Initially, Plato distinguishes six categories: the amiable and the vicious, each of whom may hold any one of the three heresies.

---

[2] The refutation of the heresies in the earlier part of the book constitutes the law's 'preface'.

These six need '*dike* (justice or penalty) which is neither equal nor similar'. However, this promisingly full analysis seems to be without penological effect: the prescription of penalties relies exclusively on the twofold distinction. Presumably any elaboration will have to be at the discretion of the judges.

### 4.3  Problem 3: eironikon, *as a description of the second type of heretic* (908e2)

*Eironikon*, 'ironic', seems to imply not mock-modesty, but a contrast with the frank outspokenness of the first heretic. The 'ironic' heretic conceals the premises of his argument, and dresses up his views in some sort of plausible reasoning which makes them sound like intellectual and religious orthodoxy. For instance, he persuades us to regard 'squaring' a god as fair, reasonable, and pious; in fact he knows (in his heart?) that it is impious. *Eironikon* thus suggests not wit or rhetorical play, but intellectual trickiness.

### 4.4  Problem 4: psychagogia, '*soul-leading*' (908b)

Some of the dissembling heretics engage in 'soul-leading'; but Plato does not define the term. Probably he means the 'bindings' or 'incantations' by which one could expect to harness against one's enemy the souls of the dead. His disapproval of this belief generates a problem for him, as we shall see.

### 4.5  Problem 5: conditions of release of the '*curable*' heretic

The amiable and merely misguided heretic is to be sent for a period of at least five years (908e ff.) to the 'reform-centre' (*sophronisterion*), which is situated near the meeting-place of the Nocturnal Council (the supreme governing body of the state). Plato words the provisions for release confusingly; but the logic of the text seems to indicate (i) that after the minimum period of five years the heretic is released not by a court but at the discretion of officials: his sentence was effectively 'indefinite'; (ii) that even after release, he is on a kind of probation.

### 4.6  Problem 6: re-education (908e–909a)

Precisely how is the amiable heretic to be reformed in the *sophronisterion*? Plato distinguishes a 'compelling' and a 'teaching' element in punishment (862d). The nature of the former is in this instance fairly clear: isolation from society, psychological pressure, and contact only with such sterling characters as the members of the Nocturnal Council, who 'associate' with them for purposes of 'admonition' and the 'safety of the soul'. Plato attempts to exploit the formative power of association. But what does the 'teaching' consist of? Readings from *Laws* 10? Daily? Monthly? Something intellectual seems called for, but Plato does not even begin to describe it. At any rate, his treatment of the amiable heretics is based on his estimate of their psychological state, and thus far he is concerned with their welfare. But the social dimension is strong: though this category of heretic inflicts less harm on society than the other, recidivism is very harshly treated, by the penalty of death.

This legislation is remarkable, and sharply different from anything in Athens, where so far as we know the impiety law did not formally distinguish psychological states (Cohen 1991: 203-17). Plato requires the top officials of his state to spend five years in reintegrating somewhat foolish persons into society; and that is consistent with his general policy of rehabilitating criminals wherever possible.

### 4.7 *Problem 7: why are the heinous heretics not killed?*

Heretics of the second class are to be imprisoned for life in a remote prison (908a, 909b-c) whose name is to be suggestive of *timoria* (vengeance). The very word suggests incurability, which would in terms of Plato's penology demand the death penalty (728bc, 862e-863a, 957e-958a). Yet they are not executed. Why? Are they residually curable in principle, but too clever for the dialectic of the Nocturnal Council? Do some of them believe at any rate in the existence of gods, so that they are not entirely beyond redemption? Or have they committed no concrete offence, but only talked? Does the line between curability and incurability lie here, between speech and action? Does Plato believe that mental states are finally assessable only by reference to acts? Perhaps he regards the mark of incurability as the solidification of fluid opinion by the habituation of action. It is after all good Platonic doctrine that one attains a certain moral character by doing actions of that character. If that is indeed his reason, we have in his heresy law a startlingly rigorous and consistent application of a moral and psychological doctrine.

### 4.8 *Problem 8: private shrines ($909^d3-910^d4$)*

Plato prescribes simply that no one is to possess shrines in private houses; for it is undesirable that shrines should be founded all over the place at the whim of persons wishing to thank or supplicate the gods for some benefit, or because of fear arising from a vision in sleep. One supposes that such practices are undesirable because they encourage a belief in a commercial, reciprocal relationship with the gods, divorced from considerations of virtue and genuine desert. A slightly obscurely written passage (910a6–b6) may suggest that such impious actions infinitely increase the impiety of impious opinions, and this lends some support to the suggestions in Section 4.7, on the relationship between belief and action.

Plato now lays down the penalties for possessing and worshipping at private shrines (910b8 ff.). There are two categories of offenders:

(1).    Those guilty of no great act of impiety, who are to be reported to the authorities, and their shrines removed to public places. Cases of disobedience are to be punished (by fines?) until the shrines are so removed. By an implication in (2), the offenders are acting childishly.

(2).    Those guilty of an act of impiety typical not of children but of adults, either by founding a shrine on private property, or by sacrificing to 'whatever gods' (foreign ones?) in public places. These offenders are to be executed, as sacrificing in a state of pollution.

The law has no counterpart in Athens, where the founding of private shrines seems to have been largely unregulated (but cf. Sect.2). Again, there is emphasis on psychology: childish acts, even if repeated, attract only repeated minor penalties, not death.

The distinction between trivial and serious offenders recalls the distinction between the amiable and heinous heretics. The problem is to know whether the lesser heretic is the same person as the childish offender, and the greater heretic the 'adult' offender. It is hard to see how the heretics who make converts by scoffing at the religion of others would be likely to found shrines; on the other hand, the serious offenders could well be (i) such heinous heretics as put their beliefs into practice, and (ii) certainly those non-childish persons who act on their teachings. The two pairs, of heretics and offenders, seem therefore to be only partly on all fours.

## 5. ASSESSMENT OF PLATO'S IMPIETY LAW

Plato's law of impiety is a highly distinctive product of his theology and moral theory. He acts within the tradition of Athenian anti-intellectual impiety legislation, but with radically different assumptions and purposes, and with a far more sophisticated analysis of heretics' intellectual and emotional states. Like Diopeithes, apparently, he is concerned not with casual or occasional expressions of heresy, but with its persistent or systematic propagation. In particular, his law seems to embody the crucial distinction between opinion and speech on the one hand, and action on the other; only the more serious actions (and the recidivist 'amiable' heretic) attract the death penalty. However religiously horrible your opinions, and however assiduously you urge them on others, you are executed only if you act on them. But although heresy seems a natural area in which a penology aiming to cure psychic states could come into its own, by deploying reasoned persuasion, the scope of the re-education envisaged by Plato is a much more limited operation than a swift reading of the final pages of book 10 would suggest. It does not touch the more dangerous type of heretic. Finally, the provisions for the release of the naïve heretic seem to embody the principles of indefinite sentence, terminable by officials rather than by a court, and of probation.

## 6. MEDICINE AND MAGIC

We now turn to book 11, and in an intriguing set of laws (932e1-933e5) we meet our old friends the magicians or charlatans of the law of impiety. They are now bracketed with malicious doctors, under the general heading of 'poisoners': just as doctors may, if they wish, poison the bodies of men directly, charlatans 'poison' them on another level, intellectual or spiritual, by a set of practices which we may compendiously call 'magic' (933a, 933cd; cf. 908d, 909b).

### 6.1 *Doctors*

The law relating to doctors is in effect a branch of the law of *blabe*, damage. It covers deliberate non-fatal poisoning of human beings, and fatal or non-fatal poisoning of certain animals. Doctors who commit either offence, by food, drink, or unguents, are to be executed; what the layman must suffer or pay is to be assessed by the court.

The Attic law of damage was of very wide application, and could probably be used in cases of poisoning; the penalty for deliberate damage would then have been restitution to the extent of double the assessed amount of the damage. At any rate, no special penalty for malicious doctors is known. Plato's law is very different; presumably he would reason as follows. A doctor has a skill, with great potential for harm; he has betrayed the trust put in him; he must therefore be incurably wicked. The layman may be an ignoramus, or partly skilled; his penalty has therefore to be open-ended. Plato thus calculates penalties on the assumption that the degree of the technical knowledge misused by the offender is a measure of his psychic vice, and therefore a measure of the punishment needed to cure him, if indeed he is curable. He makes no mention of recompense to the victim.

### 6.2 Magicians

The text contains a description of the second type of poisoning: it proceeds by trickery, charms, and bindings, and persuades both aggressor and victim of the efficacy of such practices in the infliction of harm. Two problems arise, which we may clear off briefly before considering the connection Plato makes between medicine and magic. The relevant passage reads (933a5-b5):

On these and similar matters [trickery, etc.] it is neither easy to discover how things really stand, nor, if one were to find out, simple to persuade others. It is not worth trying to persuade about such matters persons scowling at each other by the souls of men, that if some people sometimes see somewhere images fashioned from wax at doorways or crossroads or on tombs of their ancestors—to bid them ignore all such things, since/when/if/although they/we have no clear opinion about them.

### 6.3 Problem 9: what does 'persons scowling at each other by the souls of men' mean?

Probably it is a description of mutually malevolent persons, each of whom thinks that the other has incited the soul of some dead man to attack him. 'By' may thus be either instrumental (they try to use a soul), or causal, 'because of' (the souls are a cause of their suspicion).

### 6.4 Problem 10: what is the relevance of the remark about the lack of a 'clear opinion'?

It can hardly imply that Plato is uncertain whether gods are venal or not: on that issue he is immovable. It is probably a piece of rhetorical exaggeration enjoining suspension of judgement. For Plato has a problem. It is to show how, given the continuity between this world and that of the dead on which he has himself insisted in the homicide law (e.g. 865d-e), influence of the dead on the living is possible, while influence of the living on the dead, at least of the kind envisaged by magicians, must be ruled out. No doubt it could be shown; but it would not be easy to persuade others, even if one found out—and I take it Plato reports a puzzlement he really does feel. At all events, he knows that presenting such a probably subtle and complex argument to observers of waxen images is 'not worth it'; they will take the prudential option every time. The best he can do is to urge them, as he urged the young heretic earlier (888c ff.), to bear in mind that they do not have a sure opinion, and to await a more mature one.

If these solutions of the two problems are correct, it looks as if in the conjuration of the dead and related practices Plato is worried by the problem of distinguishing magic from medicine. His remarks on the way in which magic convinces both the victim and the aggressor of the reality of its effects suggest that his uncertainty centres on whether magic really works, like (some) medicine, and has the results it claims. Certainly he seems to suppose, in mentioning *manganeumata*, 'hocus-pocus', that magicianship involves some sort of technical knowledge of procedures and rituals (933c), and that in so far as the magician has or claims to have technical skills, he may as well be compared with any other expert, say a farmer or a carpenter—or a doctor.

Whatever Plato's doubts, he gives the magicians the benefit of them. The concession is, however, deadly. For it immediately puts them on the same footing as doctors: expert use of bindings and charms or other such poisons attracts the death penalty; but a non-expert magician found guilty of such poisoning attracts an open-ended punishment, like the non-expert doctor, presumably because the degree of skill he misuses similarly varies, and therefore the degree of his psychic vice.

There are a few indications that sorcery could be repressed under Attic law too, perhaps as a species of impiety. The main innovations Plato seems to have made are the subjection of magicians and malicious doctors to essentially the same law, under the general heading of 'poisoners', and the firm distinction between expert and non-expert in both categories. As best he can, as in his penal code in general, he puts the measurement of psychic states at the centre of his law.

## 7. CONCLUSION

The comprehensiveness of Plato's impiety law, and the fertility of its ideas, are remarkable. It embraces a wide variety of offences, ranging from the purely intellectual to the practical and common-place, and grades them in the light of the damage they do and the mental states that caused them. Its main analytical tools are the distinctions between speech and action, expert and non-expert, and the clever and the naïve. It is an important episode in the history of thought, and deserves to be better known.

# 7

## Lysias against Nikomachos: The Fate of the Expert in Athenian Law[1]

### STEPHEN TODD

#### 1. PRELIMINARIES

There are six preliminary questions which scholars traditionally ask about any surviving Athenian forensic (i.e. lawcourt) speech. Three of these questions concern the personalities of the trial: who wrote the speech? who was the speaker? and who was the opponent? The other three questions are about issues: what was the date of the trial? under what legal procedure did it take place?[2] and what was the result? In terms of our level of knowledge, Lysias 30, *Against Nikomachos* is a typical speech: we are neither particularly well nor particularly badly informed. Out of the six preliminary questions outlined here, we know the answer to three (subject in each case to qualification), and the other three are unknown (although we may be able to guess at the answer to one of these).

The obvious place to begin is with the title of the speech in the manuscript: it is, we are told, by (or at least attributed to) Lysias. But a lot depends here on what is meant when we use the word 'by'. We may not agree with everything that Dover says about the authorship of Athenian forensic speeches,[3] but he has certainly

---

[1] This paper was originally delivered as part of the seminar series which makes up this book, but it also draws to some extent on unpublished material previously presented to audiences in Cambridge in 1986 and in Keele in 1988. My thanks are due to numerous participants in each of the three seminars, but especially to the editors of this volume.

[2] The nature of Athenian law means that procedure is a considerably more important concept than the question of charge or offence: see Todd (1993: e.g. 64–7).

[3] See Dover (1968: 47–56); my own views on the subject of authorship have been outlined in Todd (1990: 165–7). For the sake of convenience, and because it does not substantially affect our argument, we may throughout this paper ignore what is at least the theoretical possibility that this or any other speech has been

demonstrated that we cannot use the authorship of a speech as a statement of political consistency. Lysias was a forensic orator: that is, he did not normally speak in public, but instead wrote speeches to be delivered by private individuals involved in litigation (or, as Dover would put it, he assisted these litigants in composing their speeches). Even if we could demonstrate that every word of this speech was written by the orator, with no contribution whatever from his client, nevertheless we could draw from this hypothesis no deductions whatever about any political views of the orator which underlie the speech. Lysias, as Dover has shown, was willing to work with clients from a wide range of political backgrounds— indeed, a surprisingly wide range, given Lysias' own experiences as a political refugee under the oligarchy of the Thirty.

The second piece of information given by the manuscript title concerns the opponent, where we are at least told that his name was Nikomachos. That, however, does not tell us very much, because outside this speech he is mentioned only once by a classical source. In the closing lines (1504-14) of Aristophanes' *Frogs*, produced in 405 BC, Hades god of the underworld is heard recommending various public figures to commit suicide as soon as possible:

give this [presumably some instrument capable of causing death] to Kleophon; this to the *poristai*, to Myrmex and to Nikomachos; and this to Archenomos; and tell them to hurry down here as soon as possible, or else I will brand them and tie up their feet with Adeimantos the son of Leukolophos, and hasten their passage below ground.[4]

And even with the name of the opponent, we are not entirely on safe ground: it is generally agreed that he was called Nikomachos, but at one point in our manuscript (§ 11) he is addressed as Nikomachides; and the lexicographer Harpokration (s.v. *epibole*) cites this speech under the title *Against Nikomachides*.

Concerning the date, on the other hand, we can be fairly certain. Lysias tells us that Nikomachos served two terms in office, the first of which (§ 2) lasted six years, and did not end until 'the *polis* had

mis-attributed, and that it is not 'by' Lysias but 'by' another orator; references in this paper to 'Lysias', therefore, are shorthand for 'whoever wrote the speech(es) in question'.

[4] The *poristai* were a board of public officials, but the rest of the names here are of individuals. Presumably they are all politically active: one at least of them (the 'demagogue' Kleophon) is well known and will reappear throughout this paper.

been reduced to utter disaster' (§ 3); this final phrase is a standard Lysianic euphemism (e.g. Lysias 6. 46, 16. 4, 25. 15, 31. 8) for the complex of events from the loss of the Athenian fleet at Aigospotamoi (summer 405), to the Spartan siege of Athens (winter 405–4), and the final Athenian surrender (spring 404). This six-year term, therefore, will have spanned the period from the restoration of democracy after the fall of the first oligarchy (the Four Hundred) in 411, to the rise of the second oligarchy (the Thirty) imposed with Spartan support after the surrender in 404.[5] Nikomachos, however, also served a second term, which lasted four years (§ 4). It is inconceivable that he was appointed by the Thirty, because Lysias would certainly have said so; and the natural inference is that Nikomachos was reappointed after the second democratic restoration (late summer 403). If, as we would expect, the calculation here is inclusive and based on the Athenian calendar year, then the fourth year of his second term will have been 400/399.

Once again, however, a cautionary note should be sounded. Broadly speaking, here, and particularly for the dating of Nikomachos' second term, I have followed the calculations made by Dow (1960: 271–2). But Dow (ibid. 291) further assumed that an Athenian public official could only be prosecuted at the end of his term of office, and that the speech must therefore have been written for a trial early in the calendar year 399/8. This, however, is to import assumptions from Roman constitutional law into the law of Athens: at Athens, as we shall soon discover, there were several procedures by which a sitting official could be prosecuted. So there is also the possibility that the trial should be dated in the spring or early summer of 399, towards the end of the Athenian year which began in the summer of 400. On the other hand, it is unlikely that the trial was much later than Dow believed: Nikomachos may, as Dow suggested, already have finished his term of office; but if so, that must have been a very recent event.

---

[5] 'Six years' is presumably (despite Dow 1960: 271) an inclusive reckoning on the basis of Athenian calendar years, which ran approximately from midsummer to midsummer: Nikomachos' term will therefore have run either from some time during the year 411/0 to some time during the year 406/5, or (more likely) from some time during 410/409 to some time during 405/4. We might infer from the account in §§ 10–14 that Nikomachos was still in office at the time of the trial of Kleophon in the winter of 405–4, but the fact that Lysias implicitly suggests this is no guarantee that it is true.

This, then, is the sum total of the three things that we know about the speech: author, opponent, and date. There are two things which we have no way whatever of determining: the identity (and political affiliations) of the speaker; and the result of the trial. As for the procedure, however, and by implication therefore the charges, the situation is rather more complex. The title in our manuscript speaks of *euthynai* (the judicial examination of his accounts to which every public official had to submit at the end of his term of office); but the titles of speeches in our manuscripts are not always reliable, and sometimes appear to be based on little more than dubious inferences from the text of the speech.[6] In this title, for instance, Nikomachos is described as a *grammateus* ('clerk' or 'secretary'); and although Lysias in § 27 insultingly describes him as a *hypogrammateus* ('under-clerk'), it is clear from §§ 2, 4, 17, etc., that Nikomachos' office was in fact that of *anagrapheus* (literally 'publisher', cf. below). Moreover, there is indeed one piece of internal evidence which suggests that this speech may not have been written for Nikomachos' *euthynai*. Lysias insists very emphatically at § 5 that the defendant, alone among public officials, has reached such a pitch of arrogance that he has consistently refused to offer his accounts for examination. This argument would be considerably weakened if Nikomachos could stand up and reply, 'but you now have my accounts in front of you'.

There are, moreover, two other possible procedures which must be considered here: *graphe alogiou* and *eisangelia*. The former was a public prosecution (that is, it could be initiated by any citizen) used to charge an official for failure to offer his *euthynai*, but its use is rarely attested. Better known, however, is *eisangelia*, which broadly corresponds to modern impeachment: this too could be brought by any citizen, but against any serving as well as former official, and on the basis of any form of malpractice committed in office. It was characteristic of *eisangelia* that there was a double hearing, first before the council and then either before the assembly or, more commonly, before a court:[7] our present speech is addressed to a

---

[6] There are, however, instances where the speech-title contains apparently reliable information which cannot simply have been deduced from the text of the speech as we have it, such as the name of the defendant Mantitheos in Lysias 16: cf. Blass (1887: 517).

[7] For the detailed rules, see Hansen (1975: 21–8): the cases heard by the council and then by the court are those described by Hansen as '*eisangeliai* to the council', and it is among these that he provisionally places the trial of Nikomachos (ibid.

court (§ 1), but Lysias refers in passing (§ 7) to the slanders which Nikomachos is alleged to have uttered before the council. It is an attractive suggestion that this refers to comments made at the preliminary hearing of an *eisangelia*; and this is perhaps the most likely procedure, though it is not wholly certain.

We have devoted some time to a rather inconclusive discussion of the technicalities of procedure; but the issue is important, because it raises questions of initiative and risk. If the trial of Nikomachos was either a *graphe alogiou* or an *eisangelia*, then we can deduce that the prosecutor is attempting to force the defendant's hand. If what we have is the examination of Nikomachos' *euthynai*, then this is an automatic process consequent upon the completion of his term of office, and no such inference can be drawn. In a *graphe alogiou*, as in the majority of public procedures, a prosecutor who failed to get one-fifth of the votes of the jury would suffer a substantial fine and probably also the loss of certain civic rights (at the least, the right to bring the same type of legal case in future). *Eisangelia*, however, though a public procedure, was at least at this date exempt from the one-fifth rule,[8] and even if Lysias' client had obtained no votes whatever, he would not have suffered any tangible penalty other than a loss of prestige. The status of the unsuccessful complainant at *euthynai* is less clear, but it seems probable that he suffered no penalty, perhaps because he was not formally regarded as a prosecutor. In an *eisangelia*, finally, there was a preliminary hearing before the council, and although the range of offences covered by this procedure was virtually limitless, the plaintiff would presumably have to show prima facie that the defendant had done at least something which could serve as the basis for a charge. This would be less of a problem in a *graphe alogiou*, where it is by definition clear what the charge would have

116–17, cat. 140); it is notable (cf. n. 9 below) that in such cases the council passed not simply a preliminary resolution but a preliminary verdict (*katagnosis*). Strictly speaking, Hansen's 'eisangeliai to the assembly' received more than two hearings, since they were normally initiated in the assembly, referred to the council with the instruction to place them on the agenda, and from there referred back normally to the assembly for a final hearing; but since this is not the type of case in issue here, we may take the liberty of over-simplifying.

[8] *Eisangelia* seems to have been brought into line with other public procedures in this regard in the 330s, apparently in order to reduce the threat of frivolous prosecutions: see Hansen (1975: 30).

had to be;[9] but as we shall see, it is hard to see quite what Nikomachos could be said to have done that might justify an *eisangelia*.

To our preliminary questions, therefore, we are left with the answer that we know neither particularly much nor particularly little; but a lot of the things that at first sight we seem to be able to answer conclusively turn out on closer examination themselves to raise further questions. But that is perhaps an unduly gloomy note on which to end the first section of this paper, for there is one respect in which for this speech we are in a better position than for many others: we do at least have some external evidence, and are not solely confined to making inferences from the text itself.

We have already noted the jibe against Nikomachos made at the end of Aristophanes' *Frogs*. More valuable perhaps in this case is the anonymous material. Nikomachos, as we have seen, served two terms of office as *anagrapheus* or 'publisher' of the laws, and in this task he appears to have formed part of a commission charged with revising and inscribing the law of Athens.[10] We possess substantial epigraphic fragments of work which may have been published by the commission. Some of this was completed during Nikomachos' first term of office, but the only substantial item from this period to survive[11] (the republication of the homicide law ascribed to the seventh-century legislator Drakon, *IG* I³ 104 = Meiggs and Lewis 1988: no. 86) describes itself in its prologue as the work simply of *anagrapheis*, and this may or may not denote the board of which Nikomachos was a member. More significant perhaps is the work produced during Nikomachos' second term, from which there survive very considerable fragments of a calendar listing the state

---

⁹ There was a preliminary hearing of sorts (the *anakrisis*) before every public case; but the *anakrisis* was conducted by a public official, and he may well have had less discretion (in practice even if not in theory) to reject a case than the council had over an *eisangelia*. There is some evidence that officials preferred not to take the responsibility for rejecting a case at this stage (Lysias 13. 85 7), presumably for fear of what might happen at their own *euthynai* (cf. Lysias 10. 16). The council, on the other hand, in *eisangeliai* of this sort were expected to deliver a preliminary verdict rather than simply a preliminary resolution (cf. n. 7 above).

¹⁰ The role of the *anagrapheus* is discussed in Sect. 2 of this paper, and the significance of the revision of the laws in Sect. 4.

¹¹ There is at least one other text which was evidently produced at the same time, but it is so fragmentary as to defy serious interpretation: this is a law or collection of laws apparently concerned with the powers of the council (*IG* I³ 105). For other possible texts, see Robertson (1990: 56 60).

sacrifices of Athens.[12] Neither document, however, names Nikomachos: it is not certain that the homicide law has anything to do with him; and although the calendar (cf. §§ 17–25 of the speech) is presumably to be associated with the work of his commission, nevertheless its extant fragments tell us nothing about the constitutional framework within which its authors were working.

The evidence of the inscriptions, however, brings into play some additional literary material. They make it clear that Nikomachos was playing a part in a substantial process of legal revision during the final decade of the fifth century; and several of our literary sources provide partial (in every sense) accounts of this process. Thucydides (8. 45–98) and Aristotle in the *Constitution of the Athenians* (29–33) give revealing though incompatible versions of the rise of the first oligarchy, that of the Four Hundred, in 411 BC. Both show clearly how the oligarchs were helped to power by a very considerable confusion over the nature and authority of the law of Athens: what is the value, for instance, of a constitutional safeguard to defend the position of the democratic assembly, if there is no safeguard to prevent the assembly from simply repealing that safeguard and abolishing itself in favour of an oligarchy (cf. Thucydides 8. 67)? The *Constitution of the Athenians* in particular casts an interesting if unintentional light on the way in which the question of law served as an ideological battlefield in the propaganda wars of this decade, with all parties claiming that theirs was the true 'ancestral constitution'.[13]

From a somewhat later stage in the process of legal reform, we have the orator Andokides. In the course of his defence-speech *On the Mysteries* (Andokides 1. 71–89), written for a trial probably in 400 BC (thus MacDowell 1962: 204–5), he puts forward a detailed and immensely confusing account of legal reform in Athens in the period 405–403/2. There is, as we shall discover in the final section of this paper, a strong case for believing that Andokides' account is grossly and deliberately misleading; but for what it is worth, it is additional evidence.

---

[12] The calendar has attracted a considerable specialist bibliography: in addition to the 24 specialist items noted in Dow (1960: 292–3), see more recently Dow (1961), Fingarette (1971), Clinton (1982), and Robertson (1990).

[13] The outstanding discussion of this topic is that of Finley (1986: 36–59). The implications of the first oligarchic revolution for the status of law at Athens are discussed further in Sect. 4 of this paper.

A final mention should perhaps be given to comparative material. Much of Lysias 30 is devoted to rhetoric about the law and about legal experts; and much of this can be matched elsewhere, in the speeches both of Lysias and of other orators. Comparison can help us to contextualize what may be the function of Lysias' discourse here.

## 2  THE FUNDAMENTAL PROBLEM: THE PROSECUTOR'S CASE

The main problem which scholars have traditionally found with Lysias 30 is that it is exceedingly difficult to see quite what it is that Nikomachos is charged with (Albini 1952: 266; Gernet and Bizos 1955: 160; and cf. more recently the use of 'presumably' in Hansen 1975: 117, cat. 140). This problem remains, unless we are prepared to fudge the issue by saying that he is being charged simply with 'not carrying out his functions in the way that he was ordered to'; or unless we take what I suspect is the more subtle and accurate line that in order to be found guilty in an Athenian court, you did not actually need to have done (or not done) anything in particular.

What Lysias says boils down to this. Nikomachos served two terms in office (§§ 1–6). In the first of these, described in §§ 2–3, he was appointed for a four-month period as *anagrapheus* (§ 2).[14] The significance of this word (literally, 'one who writes up') is open to interpretation. Robertson (1990: 52–6) rightly emphasizes that it could include the 'researching' of texts; but its natural meaning involves the act of writing up in a public place, and it is difficult to accept his argument that this should specifically exclude its common corollary, the inscribing of laws. It is admittedly impossible on purely linguistic grounds to determine the level of discretion which the term implies (is the *anagrapheus* simply the man with the chisel who carves the text on the stone, or does he have a real authority over the status of the text to be inscribed?); but the *Constitution of the Athenians* (30. 1, 32. 1) uses the related verb *anagrapho* to describe those charged with drawing up and publishing a constitution, which implies that such discretion could be considerable. According to Lysias, however, Nikomachos 'made himself into a

---

[14] The term *anagrapheus* is employed here specifially, in a way which makes it clear that the subsequent uses of *nomothetes* and (*hypo*)*grammateus* are for the purposes of irony or insult.

*nomothetes* (lawgiver) and made his job last six years' (§ 2). The latter, as we have seen, neatly covers the period between the two oligarchies; while the former is presumably an accusation of having exercised more discretion than he was entitled to. He 'inscribed some laws and erased others, while receiving payment on a daily basis' (§ 2): this of course is meant to sound as if he took bribes for perverting the lawcode, but it may simply mean that Nikomachos had a post for which he received a daily stipend, and that he was allowed at least some discretionary powers over the texts which he selected as authorities. Since Lysias is a master of innuendo, it is safe to assume that the words here mean no more than they say.[15] In a phrase that is delightfully vague,[16] 'the archons imposed *epibolai* (summary fines) and brought matters into the courtrooms, but he refused to hand over the laws' (in other words, the task on which he was engaged was one that took some time); and he did not give up his office and submit to *euthynai* (cf. Section 1 above) until the city was overtaken by 'disasters' (§ 3). The phrasing here implies, incidentally, that Nikomachos did eventually give up his office and undergo *euthynai*, even if this did not happen until after the defeat at Aigospotamoi in 405; and the speed of his reappointment after the democratic restoration in 403 may support the conclusion that he almost certainly did this before the fall of the democracy in the autumn of 404.

Nikomachos' second period in office is described in §§ 4-5. This time he is not formally described as an *anagrapheus*, but the cognate verb *anagrapho* is used twice in § 4 to describe his activities; and it seems reasonable to conclude that once again this was indeed the title of his office. There is some reason to believe that he dealt with a narrower range of material during this second term. The epigraphic evidence for the work of the second commission consists entirely of fragments from a sacrificial calendar; and it is possible that when Nikomachos is later said to have been in charge both of *hosia* and of *hiera* (non-sacred and sacred matters, § 25), the two

---

[15] We may note in passing that Lysias in this speech is fond of the 'inscribed some/erased others' jingle: it is repeated in almost the same words in § 5. The significance of the charge of 'erasing' laws is discussed in Sect. 4 below.

[16] There is, as Robertson (1990: 54 n. 36) complains, no warrant in the text for the assumption made by all previous editors, that it is Nikomachos who is being fined and summoned here: simply that his slow progress caused judicial delays. On the other hand, the way in which this passage has traditionally been read demonstrates Lysias' success in making it sound a very serious matter.

words refer separately to the two periods of office. In § 4, indeed, Lysias goes further, encouraging us to infer that Nikomachos' authority was statutorily circumscribed during his second term, but this may be simply a clever use of words: the phrase διωρισμένον ἐξ ὧν ἔδει ἀναγράφειν (*diorismenon ex hon edei anagraphein*, literally, 'it was defined out of what things he had to inscribe') is meant to suggest a restriction of the areas of law over which Nikomachos was to have competence, but it need mean only that he was to draw his regulations from specified sources.[17] The duration of Nikomachos' second term occasions yet more sophistry. Lysias says that he took[18] four years over a task which he could have completed in thirty days (§ 4), which is clearly meant to recall the earlier allegation (§ 2) that Nikomachos had illegally extended his first term of office; here, however, the speaker claims no statutory authority for his mention of thirty days. The decree of Teisamenos of 403, quoted by Andokides (1. 83-4), does specify this figure, and it is possible that the audience may dimly have remembered this; but although the decree of Teisamenos dealt with contemporary and related aspects of law reform, nevertheless it had no direct connection with Nikomachos' commission. We may safely conclude that the limit of thirty days here has no authority outside Lysias' imagination. This gives way to the final accusation, that Nikomachos has not submitted his accounts (§ 5). Lysias, of course, wants us to infer that such behaviour is unlawful; and he confuses the issue by drawing a contrast with 'the others' who (unlike Nikomachos) do this not just on an annual but on a monthly basis.

---

[17] The surviving portions of the calendar do specify the sources from which individual regulations are drawn (cf. the discussion by Dow 1955-7: 15-21 of the 'ek-rubrics'). The work published in the commission's first term may have been less clearly regulated in this respect: although the homicide law (Meiggs and Lewis 1988: no. 86, cf. Sect. 1 above) has apparently retained the textual divisions of the document from which it was copied and although the preface to this law instructs the *anagrapheis* 'to receive it from the *basileus* with the secretary of the *boule*', nevertheless there is no sign that the commission had a statutory obligation here to specify the source of their text. It is of course possible that, in the light of experience of the commission's first term, the assembly was more careful to specify the terms of reference for their successors.

[18] The tense of ἀνέγραψεν (*anegrapsen*) is aorist, which should indicate a completed rather than a continuing process: thus 'took' rather than 'has [so far] taken'. It need not, however, indicate that Nikomachos has voluntarily relinquished office: if (as seems probable, cf. Section 1 above) the prosecution is by *eisangelia*, the defendant will presumably have been suspended by *apocheirotonia* pending the trial; while even if the process is a *graphe alogiou*, the speaker may wish to create an impression of confidence by suggesting that the defendant as well as his job is finished.

But 'the others' is ambiguous: does it refer to Nikomachos' colleagues on the commission, or (more likely) to the holders of other, regular offices? We have no evidence external to this passage that an extra-ordinary official appointed without fixed term of office was liable to render monthly or even annual accounts during the course of his term.

This account of Nikomachos' activities in office is followed by a series of pre-emptive strikes directed against what he may say in his defence (§§ 7–16). This has only indirect bearing on the question of the possible charges, and can therefore be covered in a more cursory fashion. Three arguments are put forward. First comes the dismissal of an expected attack on the speaker's record under the oligarchy of the Four Hundred (§§ 7–8): it is perhaps significant that there is no reference to the speaker's activities under the Thirty. In the second place, Lysias attempts to rebut the defendant's claim to be a democrat (§§ 9–14). The use of the semi-technical term *mnesikakein* (§ 9: cf. the *Constitution of the Athenians* 39. 6) at the opening of this argument is made to sound as if it is Nikomachos who has taken the initiative in breaking the amnesty of 403/2, and that this therefore entitles Lysias to discuss in detail the execution of the democratic political leader Kleophon by an oligarchic kangaroo court shortly before the revolution which established the Thirty in 404; but despite Lysias' best efforts, the defendant's connection with this affair (which will be discussed in Section 3 of this paper) was clearly remote. The third argument is directed specifically against the basis of Nikomachos' claim to democratic sympathies, his exile under the Thirty (§§ 15–16), and here the logic is indeed tortuous. Nikomachos, we are told, deserves no credit for his exile, because he had no choice in the matter: as if all the victims of the Thirty, including Lysias himself, had somehow volunteered for the privilege!

There follows an extended and complex discussion of the propriety of retaining certain sacrifices (§§ 17–25). This is a particularly difficult section of the speech, not least because the text is insecure at one crucial point, and the precise meaning of several of the terms used is unclear.[19] What is interesting, however, is the importance

---

[19] *Stelai* in our editions of § 17, 'he claims that I am committing impiety by saying that we should perform the sacrifices from the *kurbeis* and from the *stelai* according to the *syngraphai* [some sort of document]', is Taylor's plausible emendation for a meaningless phrase in the manuscripts, but it has the authority only of a

given to the rhetoric of religious traditionalism, a point to which we shall return (at the start of Sect. 3 below): this discussion is allowed approximately one-quarter of the entire speech (9 sections out of 35).

After this comes a skilful and epigrammatic summary of Nikomachos' putative offences (§§ 26–30), the core of which is found in the threefold usurpation of § 27: he is a slave who has made himself a citizen, a beggar who has become rich, and a *hypogrammateus* who has arrogated to himself the function of *nomothetes*. The second of these three accusations is easy enough to decode: it is the routine forensic charge of embezzlement (for examples within the Lysian corpus alone, see 21. 16, 27. 6–7, 28. 3, and 29. 11). The other two, however, are more interesting and better developed. With the first, Lysias is picking up the offensive remarks about his opponent's family with which he began the speech. Nikomachos, we were told there, has 'treated the property of the *polis* as his own, while being himself the property of the *polis*' (§ 5, where the innuendo of slave-birth is cleverly deployed to buttress the otherwise unsupported allegation of corruption); and a series of careful hints had encouraged us to think that there was something irregular about the defendant's appearance on the citizen register and something disreputable about his upbringing.[20] In §§ 26–30, however, what had been implicit is now made overt with a series of neat puns:

if my opponent deserves to be executed on his own account, then on account of his ancestors he ought to be sold [sc. as a slave] (§ 27);

[it is a terrible thing that] you have selected Nikomachos as inscriber of our ancestral regulations (*ta patria*) when as far as his ancestry goes (*kata patera*), he does not have any share in the *polis* (§ 29).

The third accusation, however, is more difficult to understand, not least because we do not for certain know the precise significance of

conjecture. *Stelai* are 'pillars' carrying inscriptions. Nobody (even in antiquity) was sure what a *kurbis* was, but Drakon and Solon are both said to have inscribed their laws on '*axones* and *kurbeis*'.

[20] Compare the double paraleipsis (highlighted innuendo produced by omitting crucial information) in § 2: 'the age at which he was presented to his phratry' is presumably meant to imply that this had occurred at a suspiciously late age (rather than in early childhood, as was normal, cf. *P.Oxy.* 2538 col. II 23–8); 'how he disported himself as a young man' suggests the sort of sexual misdemeanours of which Lysias elsewhere accused the younger Alcibiades (Lysias 14. 25–8) and Aischines accused Timarchos (Aischines 1. 39–69).

the compounding preposition *hypo-* in the term *hypogrammateus* (lit. 'under-clerk' or 'under-secretary'). Rather than indicating a precise clerical grade, the term may instead be a way of referring to any *grammateus* who is serving as the regular subordinate to a specified official (for a possible parallel, see Antiphon 6. 35). This would serve to sustain the sophistical argument that it is illegal for a *hypogrammateus* to serve twice ' τῆι ἀρχῆι τῆι αὐτῆι (*tei arkhei tei autei*)' (§ 29). Such a law was presumably intended to prevent an individual clerk serving repeatedly as secretary 'to [successive holders of] the same office', for fear that this would become a power-base; Lysias, of course, wishes us to construe it as a ban on a clerk being continually 'in' the same office. As *anagrapheus*, however, Nikomachos does not seem to have been subordinate to a board of public officials, and the prefix *hypo-* here may therefore be deliberately insulting.

The speech ends with some brief remarks directed against those unnamed speakers who are expected to support the defendant (§§ 31–5). This of course is the regular technique of the conspiracy-theorist: if Nikomachos does come forward with supporting speakers, then Lysias has at least prejudiced the jury against them; if no suppporters appear, then the hearers' inference will be that the outspoken clarity of the prosecutor's case has frightened them into silence. Either way, the speaker has nothing to lose.

It has proved difficult in such a summary to be fair both to the speaker and to his opponent, because it has to be admitted that as the material for a charge-sheet, this does not really amount to very much. There have admittedly been some (mainly early) scholars who took at least some of the accusations at face value: Francken (1865: 205) and Gülde (1882: 3) both state as fact that Nikomachos' father was a slave; and Lamb (1930: 609–10) believes that 'his right to the citizenship . . . appears to have been doubtful',[21] studiously ignoring both the frequency and wildness of such charges in the orators and also the fact that if the speaker really believed that Nikomachos was a supposititious citizen, then

---

[21] Lamb does however admit that 'the allegation of servile birth is not clearly substantiated'. For accusations of non-Athenian birth in the orators, compare Aischines' description of Demosthenes as a Skythian (Aischines 2. 180; and cf. Deinarchos 1. 15). The procedures (and savage penalties) available for use against a non-citizen pretending to be a citizen are discussed in Todd (1993: 111, 174 n. 9, 199).

there were available several equally effective and considerably more convincing ways of proceeding against him.

The majority of scholars, however, have conceded that the speaker's accusations are at best tendentious, and that overall he had a pretty poor case. But this observation itself evokes a variety of explanations. In many ways the simplest response is to evade the problem. With the orators, it was customary among older critics to explain away the difficulties of any superficially unsatisfactory text by claiming that it was something other than the speech it purported to be. Thus Schultze (1883: 27) saw the *Nikomachos* as an epitome made by a later reader who did not fully understand what the original must have been about; and Blass (1887: 446) insisted that it was a *deuterologia*, the speech of a subordinate prosecutor in support of a principal whose work is now lost. This is the type of explanation which was supremely popular in the second half of the nineteenth century. Modern scholars are more sceptical, not least because we would tend to see problematic evidence as something that may be particularly revealing rather than something that needs to be explained away. What is striking, however, is that such sensitive critics were dissatisfied with the speech as it stands.

A more sophisticated form of evasion is displayed by the Loeb editor Lamb, when by implication he claims to detect embarrassment on the part of the orator: Lysias 'may well have felt ill at ease in attacking a man, like himself, of obscure birth, but of evident ability' (Lamb 1930: 611). This raises some interesting questions about the relationship between an Attic orator and his text; nevertheless, it cannot be accepted as a satisfactory explanation of the weakness of the speaker's case here. Lysias was a shameless man, and it is indeed difficult to think of any occasion whatever on which he was in any way embarrassed about attacking anybody.

Perhaps the most common line of interpretation among twentieth-century scholars is that exemplified by Albini, who simply dismisses the *Nikomachos* as 'a bad speech' (Albini 1952: 267). But this rests on a dangerous confusion of two very different propositions: a bad case is not the same as a bad speech. Indeed, when Lysias' arguments are analysed, as has been done in this section of the paper, it is clearly an excellent speech. We have observed for instance the repeated use of ridicule and wordplay, and the way in which ambiguous phrasing is deployed to suggest malpractice on Nikomachos' part. It requires considerable rhetorical ability to say nothing for thirty-five sections, and yet to make it sound superficially plausible at least on a first hearing. We might indeed go so far as to describe this as one of the most skilful of the speeches in the Lysianic corpus. It is also (with the possible exception of speech 13) the one in which the speaker seems to have the weakest case.[22]

### 3. THE NARROW CONTEXT: THE POLITICAL AGENDA

In order to make sense of the *Nikomachos*, perhaps the obvious starting-point is its strongly political agenda. We have already observed that more than one-quarter of the speech is given over to a discussion of pious and impious sacrifices (§§ 17–25). It is a striking fact, and one which has never been adequately explained, that charges of impiety at Athens often seem to have been highly politicized.[23] But this observation raises its own problems, for to call something 'political' is open to multiple interpretations.

When I was first asked to contribute a paper about Nikomachos to this volume, Lin Foxhall the joint organizer described him in conversation as (I cannot recall the precise words, but this is the gist) 'the small man in the middle who gets thumped by the heavies on both sides'. Now this is obviously a 'political' reading of the speech; but even though it may contain certain elements of truth, it seems to be over-romantic as a general interpretation. It is surely wrong to describe Nikomachos as a 'small man'. After all, what the speaker is complaining about is precisely that his opponent holds an exceedingly powerful position. Nikomachos is powerful because he is an expert; and yet his expertise is (ironically) at the same time his weakness: the expert, particularly the expert upstart, is both dangerously isolated and therefore hated. This is surely the under lying reason for the rhetoric about Nikomachos' slave-origins, of which we shall hear more later towards the end of this paper. To

---

[22] Judgements like this are of course highly subjective, not least because we do not know what the opponent may have said (Todd 1990: 171–2); further parallels between speeches 30 and 13, and in particular their treatment of Kleophon, are discussed in Sect. 3 below.

[23] We may think for instance of the trials of Sokrates and of Andokides, of the scandal surrounding the mutilation of the herms, and perhaps most revealingly of the case of the sacred olive-stump, in which Lysias' client makes desperate attempts to hide his politically compromising presence in Athens under the Thirty Tyrants (Lysias 7. 4, cf. 7. 9).

be an expert, and particularly to be an expert in a field which requires precise technical knowledge of a highly specialized and literate subject, is by its very nature to have undergone a lengthy apprenticeship; and yet a lengthy apprenticeship is characteristic of a slave.

The most thorough and consistent attempt to decode the political background behind the speech is that of the American epigraphist Sterling Dow, the man who has done more than anybody else to make sense of the fragmentary remains of the work of Nikomachos' commission, and who has published a series of articles specifically on the sacrificial calendar.[24] In one of these papers Dow broadened his focus to give a general interpretation of Nikomachos' work and of Lysias' speech against him; and Dow's analysis is a striking inversion of what we might have inferred from a first reading of Lysias' text. According to Lysias, Nikomachos is an enemy of the democracy and the speaker a patriotic democrat. In fact, claims Dow, Nikomachos is the democrat, who has deliberately slanted his calendar of sacrifices in favour of the common man (Dow 1960: 291, and cf. below for details), and Lysias' client is the representative of oligarchic aristocracy threatened by this attack on privilege.

Dow's is certainly a bold approach, and it draws attention to one of the things that is definitely a problem for Lysias: Nikomachos' record under the Thirty in 404/3 was clearly no more suspect than the speaker's record under the earlier oligarchy of the Four Hundred. As we have seen in our discussion of Lysias' arguments in Section 2 above, the idea that Nikomachos played any active part in the conspiracy to kill Kleophon is far-fetched, and even Lysias has to admit that Nikomachos was in exile under the Thirty. For Lysias to dismiss this as 'involuntary' is an act of desperation, especially when the speaker does not attempt to deny that he himself was in Athens during this period. Indeed, throughout the speech, and most notably at §§ 7–8 and at §§ 15–16, an evoca-

---

[24] It was Dow (1961) who first observed one of the most striking features of this inscription, that the sacrificial calendar as we have it has been inscribed on stones from which an earlier text has been erased. For a characteristically bold interpretation of this phenomenon see Robertson (1990: 65–75), arguing that it is Nikomachos' text which has been erased and replaced after our trial by one more amenable to the prosecution. Scholars have, however, traditionally believed that Nikomachos' calendar has itself replaced an earlier erasure, made either by the Thirty (Fingarette 1971) or by the restored democracy in 403 (Clinton 1982).

tive silence hangs over the speaker's own activities under the Thirty.

Despite its boldness, however, Dow's reading of the speech seems ultimately unsatisfactory. In the first place, it relies on too schematic a view of Athenian party politics: we should be very wary of any theory which assumes that there was a continuing group of oligarchic politicians operating openly in Athens in 400 or 399. Secondly, Dow's reconstruction of the case depends on his prior reconstruction of the sacrificial calendar. He believes (cf. above) that Nikomachos was being deliberately selective in his choice of material, and that he was establishing large numbers of new sacrifices in which the mass of the citizen-body could participate, while at the same time suppressing many of the traditional aristocratic rites. This is a possible but by no means proven interpretation of the calendar, and it means that Dow's reading of the speech is at best speculative. But it is the third weakness of Dow's theory that is most significant: his reading renders the speaker's position too weak to be tenable. Questions of procedure and of tactics need to be remembered here. As we saw in Section 1 above, if the prosecution was by *graphe alogiou* then the speaker stood to be heavily penalized if he failed to obtain one-fifth of the votes of the jury. No such penalty will have applied, admittedly, if we are dealing with *euthynai* or *eisangelia*. Nevertheless, if this is indeed a case of *eisangelia*, then the speaker will have needed to satisfy the council at its preliminary hearing that there was a genuine case for Nikomachos to answer—and for what it is worth, it should perhaps be noted that according to Dow (1960: 291) the putatively democratic activities of Nikomachos will have been exceedingly popular with the equally democratic council. Above all, however, whether at *euthynai* or at *eisangelia*, considerations of prestige apply. Nobody in his right mind will bring a case as weak as this against a defendant who at the time of the trial is wildly popular. It does not advance your reputation to suffer a humiliating defeat.

There is, however, a third sense, separate from the ones we have been examining, in which a speech can be labelled political: that is, that it was delivered at a time when the political atmosphere of Athens was highly charged, and with the intention of exploiting this. With this in mind, we may usefully examine in some detail the striking but rarely discussed parallels between our speech and Lysias 13 *Against Agoratos*. The latter, as we shall see, appears to be putting forward an equally weak case against a defendant who seems equally unpopular, although of course the two defendants are unpopular for very different reasons. Agoratos, unlike Nikomachos, really does seem to have been seriously compromised by his activities under the Thirty.

The most notable parallel between the two speeches is that the trial of Kleophon is discussed by both, and in broadly similar terms. Given the allusive brevity of Xenophon's passing reference (*Hellenika* 1. 7. 35), these speeches are indeed the only surviving sources to recount this event in detail. Two contrasts, however, spring to mind immediately. In the first place, the brief account in the *Agoratos* (13. 12) is less specific to the defendant against whom the speech is directed than is the version in the *Nikomachos*. For the former, Agoratos plays no direct part in the episode, in which 'they' (unspecified) packed a jury and condemned Kleophon in order to benefit those supporters of oligarchy for whom Agoratos was allegedly working. Our speech, on the other hand, has Nikomachos himself supplying the law which enables the oligarchs so to pack the jury. Secondly, for the speaker of the *Agoratos*, Kleophon is simply a democratic martyr. In the *Nikomachos*, however, he is a more problematic figure: there were, it is admitted here (30. 12), plenty of accusations which could be brought against Kleophon, but even so, his conviction was a tyrannical frame-up. This second contrast was noted by Dover (1968: 54), who proposed an explanation in terms of changes in the political temperature of Athens: the memory of radical politicians like Kleophon will have been more problematic at some times than at others. This is of course possible, but difficulties remain. What Dover does not remark is that these two speeches must have been made within a very short time of each other. The earliest possible date for the *Agoratos* is spring 399, and it was probably delivered fairly soon after this.[25] The *Nikomachos*, as we have seen, belongs at some time during 399: perhaps most

---

[25] Loening's earlier date for this speech rests on a dubious inference from Lysias' failure at 13.73 to discuss the decree giving citizenship to (some of) those metics who had assisted in the democratic restoration (*IG* II² 10, cf. T. C. Loening 1987: 74), and there is therefore no reason to reject the implication of 13.83 that this case was heard at least five years after spring 404, giving the *terminus post quem* in the text. The majority of scholars suggest a date in 400–398 (Blass 1887: 555; Gernet and Bizos 1955: 186 n. 1; Albini 1952: 93); and the reference to Strombochides, as we shall see, fits better if the *Agoratos* was heard shortly before than shortly after the *Nikomachos*.

likely is towards the end of the calendar year 400/399, which would mean the early summer of 399 itself. It has to be admitted, of course, that the political mood within a society can change very rapidly. If a week is a long time in British politics, then it will have been an even longer time in a political system like that of Athens, which had considerably more resistance to the idea of in-built delays and constitutional safeguards. But it is tempting to propose an alternative reconstruction to that of Dover to explain the relationship of the two accounts of Kleophon's trial: that the *Agoratos* was delivered slightly earlier that the *Nikomachos*; that in the latter, Lysias is adapting material which he already has on file, a general charge against those oligarchic political bosses whose activities he has previously used to blacken the reputation of Agoratos, to suit the more specific (if also more far-fetched) context of the *Nikomachos*, precisely because this material had served so well in the earlier speech; and that nevertheless, on hearing the jury's response to the *Agoratos*, he has realized that his account there of Kleophon's death had been incautiously provocative, and that the material could be more effectively deployed by making at least some concession to the ambivalence of Kleophon's reputation.

This is of course highly speculative, and the details of the relationship between the two accounts are marginal to the argument of this paper. What does matter is the fact of the relationship between the speeches, and that fact is supported by other parallels between them. In Lysias 30. 14 we are told (apropos of nothing in particular) that among other people executed by the Thirty were 'Strombochides and Kalliades'; the subject of Lysias 13 is the denunciation by Agoratos under the Thirty against one Dionysiodoros (the brother-in-law of the plaintiff, and therefore the formal subject of the case, otherwise unknown), who had been involved in a counter-revolutionary plot of which Strombochides, one of the generals, had apparently been the leader (13. 13). Now Strombochides is attested elsewhere (Thucydides 8. 15. 2, with Gomme *et al.* 1981: 37), but he is by no means a politician of the first rank. A possible inference is that the *Agoratos* was a recent (and perhaps successful) *cause célèbre* at the time the *Nikomachos* was delivered. It may also be worth noting here that these are the only two speeches of Lysias that exploit the rhetoric that the defendant is 'a slave and the son of a slave' (Lysias 13. 18, 64; 30. 2, 6, 27, 29).

Whatever the details of the relationship between the speeches, two things stand out. The two are close in date; and they are closely related. But it is the date that is perhaps most significant here: for the year 399 was, as I have myself argued elsewhere (Todd 1985: 196–99), perhaps the blackest of years for political show-trials of former supporters of the Thirty, and for breaches of the amnesty of 403/2. This is not, of course, to suggest that the *Nikomachos* is in any way an attack on the amnesty, as the *Agoratos* blatantly was. The use of *mnesikakein* at 30. 9, with its innuendo that Nikomachos has somehow himself been breaking the amnesty and should therefore experience the same treatment (cf. Sect. 2 above), is an irrelevance designed to mislead. But the political temperature of Athens was certainly high in 399; and it was this fact which will have made certain weapons particularly handy for a would-be prosecutor. And these observations may perhaps provide at least the beginnings of an explanation for what was at first sight very surprising, that Lysias was so ready to raise the topic of oligarchy even though his client the prosecutor was at least as tainted as the defendant.

### 4. THE BROAD CONTEXT: THE DISCOURSE OF LAW-REFORM

Perhaps the most interesting feature of the *Nikomachos* is the passion which the speaker devotes to the question of law-reform. As we have seen, Nikomachos' activities are to be seen either as an integral part of a general process of legal revision in the final decade of the fifth century, or at the least as closely connected with that process. Moreover, this is a process for which we have at least some contemporary evidence independent of this speech (not only Andokides 1, but also assorted inscriptions, for which see Sect. 1 of this paper). So the question can legitimately be posed: why did the Athenians in the late fifth century decide to revise their legal system, and what were they trying to achieve by this? Is it primarily a reform or a rationalization? Is the process one of codification, or is the aim simply to compile? In order to explain this, we need to look both at law itself, and at Athenian perceptions of it. Two points emerge.

In the first place, the Athenian attitude to law (especially at the popular level that underlies the arguments deployed by the orators: we may ignore here the possible existence of antiquarian scholarship) was fundamentally non-historical. There was no real conception that the past is necessarily and qualitatively different from the present, and no awareness therefore of anachronism, obsolescence, and the changing nature of institutions with the passage of time. What do you do, if as an Athenian *dikastes* (judge and/or juror) you are faced by an archaic legal statute in which some at least of the words have changed their meaning? Modern legal systems have elaborate rules of statutory interpretation. In English law, for instance, the Interpretation Act 1889 rules that unless the contrary intention appears, the term 'he' in an Act passed after 1850 must be interpreted to mean 'he or she'. Athens had no such rules, and no truly technical legal vocabulary. The language of the law was the language of the street. Consequently the Athenian answer to this problem was wholly different. Orators were not expected to discuss the original meaning of the text (indeed, it may be doubted whether they, or their hearers could have made sense of this distinction); instead, a text was to be read according to its natural and contemporary meaning. That is why, throughout the orators, anachronistic assumptions are consistently made about the rationale which underlies various pieces of legislation (eg. Lysias 26. 9; Demosthenes 18. 6, 57. 31; Hypereides, *Athenogenes* § 22). The perceived contemporary effects of the law are assumed to have been the deliberate intention of the (ancient) legislator, to the extent that on one occasion we are even told a remark allegedly made by the early-sixth-century reformer Solon when bringing a type of prosecution which we know not to have been instituted until the end of the fifth century (Demosthenes 24. 212).

There is of course one apparent exception to this rule. In Lysias 10 *Against Theomnestos*, the speaker quotes a series of archaic laws, and analyses in detail the original meaning of various apparently obsolete terms in the text. At first sight, this would seem to indicate an interest in antiquarian scholarship on the part of the orator and presumably therefore of the court; but the speaker's purpose should be carefully noted. He is prosecuting Theomnestos by *dike kakegorias*, a private indictment against slander. In his defence, Theomnestos did not apparently deny authorship of the statement that he is alleged to have made. Instead, he claimed that it was not actionable because the Athenian law of defamation penalized only the use of specified words, and did not cover what he himself had used, synonymous terms. To us, this plea would appear unusual, but it is at least possible that Theomnestos had the law on his side (thus Hillgruber 1988: 11–17), not least because Lysias' response is so brilliantly indirect. Rather than attacking Theomnestos' interpretation of the law of slander head-on, he instead proceeds to reduce it to absurdity. If words in legal texts can carry only their literal and contemporary meanings, he argues, then any law containing obsolete terms could not be applied, because such a text would no longer have any meaning; but in fact it is perfectly clear what is the contemporary equivalent for a series of terms in the texts which he is citing; therefore, it is a fundamental principle of law that words are to be interpreted to include their synonyms, thereby refuting Theomnestos' defence.

But it is important to notice where Lysias has gone for his examples here. He does not pick texts in which the meaning of the words has changed, but those in which the words are obsolete and therefore have lost their meaning. And this is surely the point: where a statute is unclear because the words no longer make sense, then if you wish to activate that text, you may decide to look for the original significance of the terms. But this will only be done for want of a better alternative, and under the stimulus of needing to win a particular argument: the hermeneutic of Lysias 10 is without parallel in the extant speeches of the orators.[26] If on the other hand the meaning of the words has simply changed, then the question does not arise. Even if an orator was aware that words do change their meanings, it would be impossible for him to convince his jury to interpret in this way a text which was already comprehensible to them in contemporary terms.

This brings us to the second point which can be made about Athenian attitudes to law: until the end of the fifth century, there was no hierarchy of norms. All legal statutes carried in principle equal authority, because *nomos* (plural *nomoi*; literally 'norm', and conventionally 'law') and *psephisma* (plural *psephismata*; literally 'that which is voted', conventionally 'decree') were formally equivalent and interchangeable terms. Any resolution of the fifth-century assembly was as such both a *nomos* and a *psephisma*. This system was changed, however, in the course of the democratic

---

[26] This may suggest that the texts in question were obsolete but formally valid (that is, they were available to be activated if any litigant so chose) rather than repealed (cf. also n. 32 below); to repeal a law is, as we shall discover, a very sophisticated concept.

restoration in 403, and *nomoi* were for the first time granted privileged status over *psephismata* (Hansen 1983: 161-77 and 179-206). Thereafter, *nomos* was restricted to rules of both general and permanent validity, *psephisma* being used to describe temporary regulations and those applicable only to individuals; no *psephisma* could override a *nomos*, and *nomoi* could no longer be changed by simple majority vote, but only by means of *nomothesia*, an elaborate and time-consuming procedure in which the assembly had no final say.

Before the first oligarchic revolution in 411, indeed, there is no sign that anybody was particularly worried about the absence of such a hierarchy. There may be some linguistic sense that rules of certain types ought to be described as *nomoi* (thus Hansen 1983: 162), but as a source of law, any statutory text was as good as any other. There was however at least a potential problem inherent in the fifth-century system: what happens when two statutes contradict each other? How indeed do you know when such a contradiction is happening? And for that matter, how do you know what the law is on any subject at all? It is dangerous to assume that there must always have been a central archive at Athens where problems like this could be resolved: indeed, the evidence suggests that when such an archive was set up in 403 in the *metroon*, the temple of the mother of the gods, this was an innovative and revolutionary step.[27] Before that date, individual public officials may have taken portable copies of particular laws which concerned their own duties, but the law itself was a text carved in stone, and before 403 such stones were scattered round the city.[28] Athenian law (cf. n. 2

---

[27] Kahrstedt (1938: 25-32) and Harrison (1955: 27-9) argued that the archive in the *metroon* was first established in 403; Boegehold (1972: 30) would want to push back this date by a few years, but not before 409. See also Boegehold (1990: 162) for a different but in certain ways parallel reading to that proposed in this paper of the complexity and potential chaos created by the scattered nature of Athenian public records in the fifth century.

[28] There is a striking indication of this in the Aristotelian *Constitution of the Athenians* 35. 2: the Thirty, wishing to annul the democratic revolution which sixty years previously had stripped its powers from the Areiopagos (the old aristocratic council of Athens), 'took down from the Areiopagos hill the laws of Ephialtes and Archestratos about the council of the Areiopagos'. This indicates first that the statute was the stone and the stone was the statute, and secondly that this particular law (and presumably it was not the only one) was itself kept in the place where it could have the greatest symbolic significance— in this case, to glare down at any nostalgic would-be oligarch on the Areiopagos who might be tempted to extend his powers.

above) was organized on the basis of procedure; and it appears that statutory inscriptions were often erected in the place where sat the court which had competence over the appropriate procedure.

Let us suppose, then, that you are a public-spirited and/or litigious Athenian of the fifth century, and you think that the activities of a political opponent may be potentially treasonable. How do you discover the existence of a statute appropriate to your opponent's alleged behaviour, given that there are lots of courts with competence in such matters? You would start perhaps by looking for the law of *eisangelia*, and guessing that it was kept near the office of the *thesmothetai*, the six junior archons. Alternatively (if your opponent held public office and you were prepared to wait until the end of the year), you could search out the law regulating *euthynai*, which you could expect to be kept near the office of the competent officials, the *euthynoi*. Or if you suspected that you could pin a charge of financial mismanagement also, you could examine one of the laws setting up either the *graphe doron* (acceptance of bribes) or the *graphe klopes* (theft, probably from public funds). The possibilities were almost limitless.[29]

What would happen, however, if two litigants produced contradictory laws, proposing different procedures or penalties, or offering rival interpretations of a central issue?[30] How, in such a situation, should the court decide to which law they should accord superior authority? In theory, this could have been done by means of a hierarchy of statutes, but as we have just seen, such a system had not yet been established. Alternatively, the court could have had recourse to the criterion of comparative dating: a case could in principle be argued that greater authority should be accorded either to the later law (because it more closely accords with current thinking) or to the earlier one (on the grounds that age confers authority). The system of legal revision established after 403 to cope with the newly privileged status of *nomoi* suggests that given the choice the Athenians would have preferred the latter option. Under the

---

[29] *Eisangelia* and *euthynai* are discussed as possible contexts for Lysias 30 in Sect. 1 of this paper. For the existence and function of alternative methods of prosecution, see the discussion by Osborne (1985) of the 'open texture' of Athenian law.

[30] This is presumably the situation which underlies § 3 of our speech. Part of the function of Nikomachos' commission was to iron out such discrepancies, and it is therefore not surprising that before they had completed their task, 'rival litigants produced contradictory laws in the lawcourts, both sides insisting that they had received them from Nikomachos'.

fourth-century rules of *nomothesia*, a new *nomos* could not be proposed unless all contradictory *nomoi* were simultaneously repealed.
This, however, is not evidence for fifth-century practice. Indeed, the
epigraphic evidence seems to suggest that it was not until the last
decade of the fifth century (and the change here may have been a
significant and even a deliberate reaction to the events of 411) that
Athenian statutory inscriptions began regularly to record in their
prescripts the name of the archon and thereby to identify the year
of enactment.[31] Under such circumstances, the criterion of comparative dating would have been wholly impracticable.

For most of the time, of course, it mattered little that an
Athenian *dikastes* could not identify the date at which a particular
law had been passed, because the role of law in an Athenian trial
was very different from that in ours. It was not the function of the
court to determine or even to know the law. Instead, it was the
privilege of the litigant, if he so wished, to bring forward any text
or texts which might support his case. If two litigants bring contradictory laws, then it is the task of the *dikastai* to decide, on the
basis of the litigants' arguments, which of the plurality of available
norms best suits the particular case. This is why there was usually
(at least before 411) no need to repeal laws at Athens: rather than
searching out a law to repeal it, you simply pass a new and different one.[32]

There are, however, particular situations in which this situation
can create problems. The most notable was the rise of the first oligarchy in 411, by means of a coup which was considerably abet-
ted by chaos and confusion over what the law actually was: which
statutes were valid, which were still valid, which carried greater
validity than others, and could they be legally invalidated? The oligarchs came to power, as we saw in Section 1 of this paper, by per-
suading the assembly to vote itself out of existence. To facilitate

---

[31] For the problem, cf. Rhodes (1981: 308). The *grammateus* (secretary), the *epis-
tates* (chairman), and the tribe in prytany (who formed an executive committee of
the council) play a part in each assembly-meeting and so are regularly mentioned
in fifth-century legislative inscriptions; the archon, on the other hand, even though
as the eponymous official he would serve to date the text, has no status within the
proceedings of the assembly.

[32] Repeal of statutes before 411 is not unknown (Thucydides 1. 140. 3 consid-
ers the possibility of annulling the Megarian decree), but seems to be considered only
in special circumstances: this is an additional reason (cf. n.26 above) for supposing
that the laws quoted in Lysias 10 are obsolete but valid rather than formally
repealed.

this, they first abolished the procedure of *graphe paranomon*, the public indictment against the proposer of an illegal decree. It is striking that this was the only constitutional safeguard which they needed to overthrow, and that it could itself be so easily repealed (Thucydides 8. 67. 2).

It was presumably this bitter experience which provided a substantial part of the impetus behind the decision to formalize the status of Athenian law in the decade from 411, a process which culminated in the establishment of a hierarchy of statutes (and thus of firm constitutional safeguards for the democracy) in 403.[33] The scale of the previously existing chaos can be inferred from the fact that nobody in 410 seems to have guessed how long the project would take. Nikomachos and his colleagues were instructed to complete their task in four months and it took six years. By 403, on the other hand, the Athenians had had enough experience not to set formal limits. But the process of reform is a complex one, which itself raises several important questions: how far was this an attempt to codify the law (i.e. to produce a single and coherent text which should supersede all other sources of law)? and if such an aim was intended, to what extent was the attempt successful?

The aim and scale of the reform is a difficult question with a range of possible interpretations. The chief problem is that Andokides 1, our main narrative account, is deliberately misleading. The reason for this deceit is clear enough. Andokides, it appears, was in a peculiar legal situation after the amnesty of 403: he was accused in 400 of breaking a ban on his participation in public religious activity, a ban which had itself been imposed by the decree of Isotimides fifteen years previously because of his participation in a major religious scandal. But because his formal offence was committed not in 415 but in 400, he was not apparently protected by the amnesty itself. (He was in fact acquitted, presumably because the court accepted his plea that it was wrong to activate a law imposing a continued sanction because of actions which he had allegedly committed before the amnesty.)

It is not, therefore, in Andokides' interests to be too scrupulous or explicit in his analysis of the legal situation. What he does is to subsume the amnesty itself into a much wider process, to create the

---

[33] See, however, Finley (1986: 35–40), for additional reasons why the discourse over the status of law was already on the agenda.

illusion of a grand process of reform in which all was to be new (Andokides 1. 71-89). This begins with the unification of Athens after Aigospotamoi (*sic*) in four stages (§ 73): (*a*) the decree of Patrokleides (405/4) reinstating those subject to *atimia* (disfranchisement: decree analysed in §§ 73-6 and quoted at §§ 77-9); (*b*) the recall of unspecified exiles, which, given the date (405/4), can only refer to the Spartan command to recall Kritias and his fellow oligarchic revolutionaries (§ 80); (*c*) the decision *me mneiskakein* (403/2, § 80, the sole and passing reference to the amnesty itself); and (*d*) the decree of Teisamenos (403/2, the background to which is analysed at §§ 81-2, and the text quoted at §§ 83-4). After this comes a series of supporting laws supposedly passed to consolidate this process: (*e*) a law banning the use of 'unwritten *nomoi*' (quoted § 85, with specious analysis at § 86); (*f*) the distinction between *nomoi* and *psephismata* (quoted § 87); and (*g*) a law defining the status of previous legal decisions and legal texts (selectively quoted § 87).

The main problem with this excursus is that our reading of Andokides' texts is necessarily conditioned by the contexts in which he supplies them. In one case, for example, we happen to possess in Demosthenes 24. 42 a fuller version of the law quoted at item (*g*), and this shows that Andokides' quotation here is selective and distorting. We have also to allow for the possibility of specious analysis, as at item (*e*), where he boldly asserts that the ban on a magistrate applying an 'unwritten *nomos*'[34] thereby necessarily invalidates an 'unwritten *psephisma*' like the decree of Isotimides. But what are we to make of his central text, the decree of Teisamenos, and his discussion of it at item (*d*)? The decree itself includes provision for (some) laws to be revised or proposed in a way that involves their being written up on a wall. Andokides himself claims that when the finished version had been properly tested it was published 'in the *stoa*' (colonnade). Scholars have traditionally interpreted this as evidence for legal codification (thus e.g. MacDowell 1978: 46-8). On this view an 'unwritten law' for the purpose of item (*e*) would be one that had not been incorporated into the new code; all the laws (*nomoi*) were to be inscribed together on the wall of 'the *stoa*' (presumably the *stoa* of the

---

[34] Does this also prevent a litigant from citing such a law, or a court from listening to it? We have no way of telling.

*basileus*[35]), and once erected this was to become the coherent and exclusive source of law at Athens; decrees (*psephismata*) were to retain their validity outside the code, but they would not be allowed to contradict it.

This orthodox picture has however been criticized by several scholars, most notably in a wide-ranging paper by Robertson (1990), who calls into question not simply the scope of codification (as does Clinton 1982), but its very existence. For Robertson (1990: 46-9), the crucial phrases in the decree of Teisamenos refer not to the permanent inscription of the whole body of law, but to the temporary posting of individual statutes being considered for revision. This is a bold reading of the text, and it may be correct, though Robertson does seem driven in places to overstate his case, perhaps because his arguments are so tightly interconnected. He ignores for instance the widely canvassed possibility that when the decree states that Athens is to use the 'laws of Solon' and 'of Drakon', these phrases denote 'the laws of Athens currently in force', or in other words texts which may already have been subjected to revision and/or publication by the *anagrapheis* during their first term. He tends perhaps to play down the broad context of legal reform in Athens from 410, as evidenced by the appointment of *anagrapheis* and by the new rules of *nomothesia* granting privileged status to *nomoi* over *psephismata*. And perhaps most significant: however persuasive Andokides was as an orator, it is hard to see how his audience would have reacted to his remarks about a general scrutiny of the laws (§ 82) and about the publication together of those that had been approved (§ 85) if, as Robertson's argument requires, these were not simply exaggerated distortions of reality, but assertions which bore no resemblance to a process in which if it had happened, they themselves would have participated no more than three years previously.

Let us for the moment therefore tentatively assume that some sort of codification was at least attempted, and see where that leads us: to what extent could this process have succeeded? The institution of *nomothesia* (cf. above) may be relevant here; this was the

---

[35] The *stoa basileios* was the traditional location of the *axones* and *kurbeis* (whatever these were, n. 19 above) containing the laws of Solon (Aristotle, *Constitution of the Athenians*, cf. Rhodes 1981: 134-6). The homicide law (Meiggs and Lewis 1988: no. 86, lines 7-8, cf. Sect. 1 above) had already been erected there; and this is where scholars have generally located the sacrificial calendar put up by Nikomachos' commission.

system introduced in 403/2 to replace a simple vote of the assembly as the way of enacting new *nomoi*. To pass a new law is to change the existing ones, and it is significant that the need for this was envisaged (if discouraged by the complexity of the procedure) at the moment when *nomoi* were first granted privileged status. Still more important is the fact that *nomothesia* was itself repeatedly emended throughout the first half of the fourth century. The details are obscure and heavily disputed (MacDowell 1975: 73-4; Hansen 1980: 87-8; Rhodes 1984: 60; Hansen 1985: 359-60), but the general effect seems to have been to make it progressively easier to change the law; and an increasing readiness to do this would be a public admission that codification had frozen the law in an artificial and unacceptable way. And of course, if indeed the laws were inscribed on a wall and not even on free-standing stones, then to emend the code would have created major physical difficulties. Unlike a word-processed typescript, an epigraphic text does not automatically re-format itself.

Hansen (1990: 70-1) has observed that there are after 399 no references in our literary sources to the 'laws in the *stoa basileios*', as the putative code would presumably have been described. At first sight, we might be tempted to respond, 'what sort of references should we expect?' But certainly if there was a process of codification, this ought to be the source of the laws cited in the extant fourth-century speeeches. Unfortunately, however, the majority of citations in the orators do not specify their physical provenance: they are usually introduced simply as 'law' or 'this law' or 'the next law' (sc. probably in the file of copies which the orator has provided for the clerk, rather than on the original stone). But there are some exceptions, and it is striking that these are not from the *stoa basileios*. Lysias 1. 30, for instance, quotes a homicide law 'from the *stele* (free-standing stone) on the Areiopagos'. The date of this speech is uncertain, and may be as early as 403: it is of course possible, therefore, that it was delivered before the passing of Andokides' 'unwritten *nomos*' law (= item (*e*) above). On the other hand, it is striking that a very similar phrase is used half a century later in Demosthenes 23. 22: 'the *nomos* from the *nomoi* about homicide from the Areiopagos (*ex Areiou pagou*)'.[36] And lest

---

[36] There is an interesting conflict here with the preface to the homicide law in Meiggs and Lewis (1988: no. 86, lines 7-8 cited above), which insists that this text is to be erected in front of the *stoa basileios*.

this should be dismissed as a peculiarity of homicide law, we may perhaps add the reference in Demosthenes 59. 76 to a law concerning the wife of the *archon basileus*, which was written (we are told) on a *stele* kept at the sanctuary of Dionysos in the Marshes.

If therefore codification was indeed attempted in the form which scholars have traditionally accepted, perhaps the most attractive explanation of its failure would be the following. Codification had been enthusiastically accepted as an ideal in 403, as a way of countering the perceived problems of chaos and incoherence created by contradictory laws. But codification inhibits change, of the type that is necessary in any society because of changing circumstances. What is more, codification makes change blatant. It had been easy before 411 to change the law without this being obvious, because all you had to do was to enact a new law. After 403, however, change would have been forced into the open. Every minor alteration to the code would have made explicit the fact that your society was no longer the same as that of your ancestors; and to become aware of this for the first time can be disconcerting. When it came to the crunch, we might suspect that the Athenians collectively preferred chaos and a sense of continuity to coherence at the price of admitting change. But if so, they never acknowledged to themselves that they were doing this: codification was never annulled, but simply dropped. And this might indeed provide us with a context for the rhetoric of the unchangeability of law. Such rhetoric is already implicit behind Lysias' repeated jingle in the *Nikomachos* (§ 2, § 5, cf. n. 15 above) that the defendant 'has erased some laws and inscribed others', which is effective precisely because for a virtuous citizen to erase a law is inconceivable. But it may be significant that it is the later orators, Demosthenes and his contemporaries from the 350s onwards, who exploit to the full the claim that the law is by its nature unchangeable. The whole point about Demosthenes' famous story about the perils of proposing new laws in the *polis* of Lokris (Demosthenes 24. 139–42, where an unsuccessful proposal results in the execution of its proposer) is that law is good and legislative change is bad, and that the prevention of legal change is the sign of a decently governed state (*polis eunomoumene*: contrast by implication Athens); and this is only the most striking of a lengthy catena of similar sentiments (Lykourgos 1. 75; Aischines 3. 37; Demosthenes 20. 104, 22. 25, 24. 5).

We return finally to the person of Nikomachos himself. It will by now have become clear that legal revision is a highly skilled task, requiring considerable expertise. But Athenians dislike experts. The point of the language about *hypogrammateis* and slave-birth (for which see Sect. 2 above) is that expertise is the characteristic of the slave, because it can only be acquired through a lengthy apprenticeship. Knowledge, of course, is power; and to be an expert in law is to have a threatening access to political patronage. This may, incidentally, be one of the reasons why it was slaves at Athens who formed the nearest equivalent to a permanent civil service: the aim was to limit the power of the specialist by isolating and marginalizing him. Since a slave could not be an independent political force, it was less risky to have slaves than to have citizens in those few permanent posts which were required. A slave's career could if desirable be easily terminated, because it was in nobody's interests to protest. It is in this context, indeed, that Lin Foxhall may have been correct (see the start of Sect. 3 above) to see Nikomachos as the figure in the middle who is attacked from all sides: he is the expert who has reached a dangerous eminence; dangerous because he is isolated; isolated because he has risen by means of his expertise, and without the customary networks of political support.

We saw at the outset that we do not know the result of the trial. But if Nikomachos did lose, despite the fact that the prosecutor's case against him was as weak as we have seen it to be, then we may now be able to see why; or at least, to see why the threat that he faced was indeed a serious one. His would have been the fate both of the 'expert' in Athenian law, and more specifically of the 'expert in Athenian law'.

# 8

## The Law and the Lady: Women and Legal Proceedings in Classical Athens

### LIN FOXHALL

### 1. INTRODUCTION

The title of this paper is derived from Wilkie Collins's virtually unknown legal thriller, *The Law and the Lady*. In Collins's novel the heroine persistently accumulates sufficient evidence to change a Scottish verdict of 'not proven' to 'not guilty' in the case of her husband, accused of murdering his first wife. True love, of course, wins out. But though the plot turns on a peculiarity of Scottish law (the possibility of delivering a verdict of 'not proven'), it derives its real interest and poignancy from the brave struggle of a woman in a man's world of detection and lawcourts.

Hence my appropriation of Collins for the title of this paper, for in classical Athens lawcourts undoubtedly belonged to the world of men. For some (Cohen 1987; Schaps 1979) that is the end of the story, and women are perceived simply as having no legal rights, though even more subtle pictures of ancient social life (Cohen 1991: 41–97) leave no place for women in the world of the lawcourts. But, as Just (1989: 28) has also recently noticed, there are a lot of women about in surviving lawcourt speeches. There is a further problem, too, in understanding the relationships of women to legal proceedings in classical Athens, and that is the 'location' of law itself in Athenian social life (and even political life, in a broad sense), and the meanings of law in Athenian world views. This problem has not been tackled by scholars of Greek law because for most the answer is 'obvious'—law was 'very important' and meant more or less the same thing it does in our society. That is, Athenian law consisted of fairly straightforward rules which (*a*) governed people's behaviour and (*b*) served as an impartial standard against which norms were established and disputes were settled. Women's lack of involvement has therefore been understood as (*a*) indicative of their lack of involvement in communal life in general (or at least the bits that 'really' mattered), (*b*) their derivative familial identities (as opposed to the personal, individual identities of men) (Just 1989: 27, Schaps 1977, 1979), and (*c*) their status as passive victims of male affairs (see Just 1989: 29). For classical Athens I am not at all sure any of this is 'obvious' or true, and the problem provides an interesting case-study for a larger issue within social theory, that of the location of law and the meaning of 'legal' behaviour in societies other than our own.

This paper, then, will be concerned with two different but related issues. The first is really an anthropological problem: is 'law' a valid category of behaviour to apply to societies other than our own, and if so, what does it mean? The second issue, the relationships of women to legal procedure in classical Athens, can only be addressed in the context of the first. My primary contention is that if it is assumed that 'law' means more or less the same thing in classical Athens as it does to us, then it would appear that women are irrelevant to legal processes. But if we question whether law is 'located' in the same places as for us, whether legal behaviour has the same or different aims, and whether legal structures integrate differently with other social and political structures than in our modern world, it becomes less easy to discount the actions of women.

## 2. OTHER PEOPLES' 'LAW'?

Once upon a time in anthropology, the study of 'primitive law' was a theoretical motorway, with many famous travellers cruising on it: Meyer Fortes, E. E. Evans-Pritchard, Lucy Mair, Max Gluckman, Paul Bohannan, and so on. Now it has become a quaint, grassy byway of anthropological theory, and the pathway peters out with S. Roberts (1979). The reason for this is that anthropologists' ideas about how societies work have changed since the heyday of structural functionalism. Under the influence of social theories inspired by structuralist, post-structuralist, and post-modernist thought, the idea that social behaviour is 'regulated' by 'norms' and 'rules' which are obeyed or contravened has for the most part been bypassed by anthropologists. Norms are seen as something to be manipulated within a larger social environment, by actors within a 'habitus' (in the terminology of Bourdieu 1977, 1990), not as regulators of collective behaviour.

For the study of so-called 'primitive law', this has created a problem. If society does not consist of rules and norms, then what significance does formal law have in societies where it exists? And does it exist at all in 'stateless' societies? For the most part the problem has been evaded in recent years either by ignoring the existence of formal law (even when 'stateless' societies are embedded within modern nation states), or explaining it away as a colonial intrusion, that is, systems which have been externally imposed on the Third World by the West (see, for example, the currently popular view that African 'customary' law was largely a construct of and reaction to colonial control).

Marilyn Strathern (1985) has produced a sophisticated, well-argued explication of arguments which are often only fuzzily implicit in the work of other anthropologists. This thought-provoking article also highlights the problem of trying to apply a category of behaviour like 'law' to a society other than our own, and this has important implications for considering the meaning and location of what we call law in the ancient world. The core of Strathern's argument is that anthropologists have seriously misunderstood dispute settlement processes, 'customary law', and other kinds of publicly expressed norms when they have construed them as something analogous to our own concept of law. For us, law is a regulatory mechanism, separable as a category of behaviour from other aspects of life, with peacefulness and orderliness as its goal. Inherent in this notion of law is the assumption that a static state of peace and order is the ultimate aim of society. While this assumption might be valid for our society, Strathern argues, it is not valid for other societies (especially 'stateless' societies), and she uses her work among the Hagen people of Papua New Guinea as a counter-example.

Strathern suggests that two notions inherent in modern, Western state societies, especially in Western social science, are responsible for anthropologists' misapprehension of primitive law. The first is that 'parts of life are seen to offer commentaries on other parts' (Strathern 1985: 112). In other words, because some behaviours or aspects of social life are perceived as descriptive of other behaviours or aspects of social life (in her words, providing a commentary), the description can be isolated from the behaviours so described without affecting the described behaviours. Described behaviour is thus a finished chapter, no longer in continuum with its description, but detached from it. For anthropologists the study of symbolism is the prime example of the detachment of 'commentary' (that is describing behaviour = the symbol) from described behaviour (what is symbolized), but law provides another instance of the separation of commentary from described behaviour (i.e. the recounting of a dispute in a formal context can be—in our terms—separated from the past and future events of the dispute itself).

The second notion, which follows on the first, is that behaviour in other societies is treated by social scientists as if it were hierarchized, with one set of behaviours perceived as shaping and controlling another. That is, norms expressed in dispute settlement procedures are understood by Western observers as defining and regulating other aspects of life, in the way that we often understand laws in our society to operate.

Strathern maintains that neither of these two notions, (1) 'privileged' behaviour as commentary and (2) behaviours as hierarchized, is appropriately applied to Hagen, for whom conflict, not peacefulness, represents the desired social end. This conflict largely expresses male collective behaviour, and certain kinds of relationships or non-relationships with other men. Public 'dispute settlement' processes are only one arena in which male conflict is expressed: the endemic tribal warfare traditional in much of Papua New Guinea is another manifestation. Dispute settlements (in which legal/moral norms are publicly expressed), she argues, have more to do with the creation than the elimination of discord. They provide an arena in which men can push their luck with people with whom they do not have a proper exchange relationship, and hopefully make themselves look good at another's expense. Moreover, the public gathering at which the dispute is aired is not separable from the events of the dispute itself, much less from future conflict (such as inter-village raids) which may ultimately result from it—it is only one, unprivileged, part of the ongoing flow of normal social conflict. Although women most certainly become caught up in social conflict, the norms expressed in public dispute procedures have little relevance to them, since this is an arena in which women play no part. Hence, Strathern argues, there is no hierarchical relationship of authority between publicly expressed norms and the domestic lived reality of women and men.

Although much of Strathern's argument is persuasive, she has formulated it as too stark a contrast between 'us' and 'them'. The anthropological opposition of the culture which is the object of study with an undifferentiated modern West is a kind of vestigial structural dichotomy that has got left behind in a world of postmodern theory. This approach precisely does *not* account for the kinds of societies we study in the ancient world, which are neither modern, nor Western, nor 'primitive'.

The states of the ancient Mediterranean and Near East bear little relation to modern states. None the less, the formal, structured behaviours which we identify as 'law' in ancient societies in most cases really are analogous to what we mean by 'law' in modern Western Europe or America. For Greek city-states, is is clear that legal behaviour does stand in a hierarchical relationship to other behaviours, and does shape lived life, although not in the same ways or perhaps to the same extent as for us. Law is much more than norms expressed in one kind of public arena, with these norms having little relevance to the rest of social life, as Strathern asserts for Hagen.

But it is undoubtedly the case that Strathern's other propositions do apply to the location, integration, and aims of legal discourse in Greek city-states. I would argue (though not in detail here) that social regulation and harmony was not the chief aim of legal behaviour as it was practised in classical Athens (as opposed to the way in which it may have been ideologically construed). Lawcourts were one of a number of arenas in which males competed with each other, often on behalf of their households (to whom this arena might not be directly accessible). Disputes could be created specifically to be played out here for the sake of competition. Moreover (and this is where the role of women becomes significant), behaviour in a court of law both instigated and manifested relationships and/or non-relationships among the opposing parties and their supporters. It was not a detached description of behaviour that was a finished chapter. The trial was only one stage of a larger social process in which continuing conflicts and alliances were expressed, and it was fully expected that these would also be acted out in the future in other arenas as they had been in the past. Women frequently had major roles to play in the pursuit of conflicts and competition in these other arenas. But in contrast to Hagen, they cannot be perceived as irrelevant to lawcourts, precisely because a hierarchical relationship between legal and other social and political behaviour *does* operate in this society. I would argue, then, that for classical Athens legal action is not merely 'descriptive' of other behaviours and thus detachable from other aspects of social life, but it does stand in a hierarchical relationship to them. To use Clifford Geertz's terminology, laws 'do not just regulate behaviour, they construe it' (Geertz 1983: 215).

Geertz's attempt to approach comparative law (1983), like Strathern's work, reflects the unease felt by anthropologists over the last ten years or so in dealing with legal systems, and discontent with past functionalist approaches to this area of enquiry. In one important regard Geertz is of more interest to those of us studying the ancient world than Strathern, for he is most concerned with legal systems in Morocco, Bali, and Java, societies which, like classical Greece, are neither primitive nor modern nor Western. Hence he does not divide the world into 'us' and 'them' in quite the way that Strathern does, but argues for a plurality of meanings of law and a variety of culturally specific locations for legal action.

Geertz's main interest in law is as a symbolic system (a slip into the anthropologist's behaviour-as-commentary mode of the kind that Strathern rightly criticizes), and as a performance of a socially constructed cosmology. Hence his entry-way into law is via keyword concepts: *haqq* in the Islamic world, *dharma* in the Indic world, and *adat* in Malaysia (analogous to terms in Greek like *nomos*, 'law, custom' and *dike*, 'justice'). His analysis is consequently heavily semantic, semiotic, and ideological. His main point is the different ways in which three cultural interpretations of law, the Islamic, the Indic, and the Malaysian, connect 'fact' and 'law'. For Geertz, 'fact' is action as expressed in the indicative mood ('as/therefore'), while law is life as expressed as conditionals, in the subjunctive ('if/then'). Law, he argues from this viewpoint, is one facet of a cosmology, which, because of its cosmological significance, formulates (and does not merely reflect) other aspects of social life. While this approach locates law firmly in relation to cosmologies and ideologies, it falls short when it comes to locating the habitus of law, i.e. its everyday, lived-out relationship to the rest of social life. This approach masks the fact that the ideology and expressed principles of law in the abstract may be very different not only from the praxis, but also from the ramifications, of legal behaviour. And founding and finding law in expressed moral principles encourages his assumption that order and harmony are the genuine intended aim of legal systems (though he certainly questions the notions that law is about 'rules' or 'dispute settlement'). Also, by perceiving law through expressed moral principles and ideals he has also enhanced the notion that law belongs to men, thus downplaying the role of women.

Geertz's approaches have been more fully and rigorously developed by Rosen (1989, 1983), who has studied the workings of Islamic law 'on the ground' in Morocco from the point of view of being an anthropologist as well as a full-fledged American lawyer. He too shies away from the notions of 'dispute settlement' and 'social control'. Like Geertz, he seizes on the relationship between 'fact' and 'law', pointing out that (1) legal decisions can be creators of 'fact', and (2) notions like 'fact' and 'truth' have culturally specific 'common-sense' definitions. Since one culture's common sense is not the same as another's, concepts like 'justice' and 'truth' must also be culturally specific.

Rosen argues that in Islamic Morocco there are three groups of concepts which locate law as a part of culture. First is the notion of *'aqel* and *nafs*—reason and passion. These are qualities inherent in all adult humans, though men 'naturally' incline toward the former and women toward the latter. Second is the notion of origins, *asel*, origins/patrimony/descent, which locates where one belongs in the social world. Third is the notion of *haqq*, which we have already met with Geertz, 'right, duty, truth, reality'.

Law in general, he argues, is like religion: 'a kind of metasystem which creates order in a universe that is often experienced in a more disorderly way' (Rosen 1989: 17). Law is founded on notions of bargaining and contract which, he argues, pervade social life. The near reduction of law to behaviours of bargaining and contract highlights the implication that the goal of law is systemic harmonious normality.

Paradoxically, this analysis mirrors Strathern (1988) and other anthropologists (e.g. Herdt 1987) in their near-reduction of Melanesian public rhetoric and other behaviours to exchange relationships. It is clear that bargaining and contract are core cultural concepts in the Islamic world, as is exchange in Melanesia. As specially significant and pervasive metaphors they may also descriptively construe behaviours. But I am uneasy with the understanding that they explain behaviours, or that they can be used to 'locate' law.

The general point of this very over-extended preamble is that neither anthropological theories of law nor empirical studies of law in classical Greece have satisfactorily explained what law is really all about in Athens in the fifth and fourth centuries BC, though Todd (1993) has gone a long way toward filling that gap on the classical side. The much smaller point I want to make here is that the roles played by women in exclusively male legal structures, and the significant role of legal action in womens' lives, highlight the inadequacy of both classical and anthropological explanations for the meaning and location of law in that society. As we shall see, it should not be assumed that women were only passive victims of men in the world of law. Of course law in Athens was about exclusion, not only of women, but of many others who were not male citizens. None the less women are there. The precise ways in which women impinge on the legal arena in classical Athens is the subject of the remainder of this paper.

### 3. WOMEN AND THE LAW

Women confronted legal structures in Athens, both as objects and as subjects, in a number of different ways. For convenience I shall discuss them under four headings (though this is an over-simplification). First and most fundamentally, women of citizen status had a legal status which could be called into question. Although these women had a political persona (without the right to exercise it, of course), the legal aspect of this political persona was essential in creating the political status of their households, their sons and daughters, and upholding the citizen status of other male relatives and affines. Hence women are frequently mentioned in cases where legitimate birth and/or citizen status is challenged.

In [Demosthenes] 59 (*Neaira*), for example, an alien woman is accused of passing her children off as legitimate Athenians, and this implicates the man cohabiting with her, who is the real target of the accusers. However, in Demosthenes 57, the speaker spends much time defending his mother's legitimate citizen status, most obviously to defend his own citizen status, but also for the sake of her honour as well. Similarly in Aischines 2. 172–3, the citizen status of Demosthenes' mother is called into question, thus implying that Demosthenes' own citizenship is doubtful.

From the lawcourt speeches we only have the men's side of the story. But in a world in which households competed with each other constantly for social and economic advantage, it must have been the case that the women took such accusations to heart as much as the men, and that they were used as weapons against other women in female networks. For example, some sacrifices, festivals, and religious offices and duties were only open to women of citizen status and/or of untainted character, so women whose citizenship or reputation was dubious would have been personally and directly affected. Such disparaging courtroom allegations would not have been felt only by the men in their lives. I have no doubt that such women would have used any means within their power to clear their names. Hence, such contentions about women in court must have had considerable ramifications for women's lives and relationships outside the courtroom. A good example of this appears in [Demosthenes] 59, where the daughter Neaira, a woman of ill repute, is disgraced by having her marriage to the *basileus archon* (the chief religious magistrate of Athens) dissolved because she is deemed not to be of citizen status. This must also call into question the assertation that women's social identities were in some way more 'derivative' of household and family than men's.

The second most obvious way that women appear in court (literally in this case) is when they have been accused of committing a crime. Not surprisingly, this is rare, since it was neither a position in which women wished to find themselves nor one in which their men wanted them to appear. The best-known cases are [Demosthenes] 59 (*Neaira*) and Antiphon 1 (the wicked stepmother), but other cases are attested (e.g. Demosthenes 57. 8). And the corollary of the undesirability of the situation is that accused women are brutally treated by their opponents in court. Women who are not on trial can also be subject to brutal accusations from their legal opponents or those of their menfolk. Apollodoros' slander of his own mother, Archippe ([Demosthenes] 45) when she chose to support her younger son and her husband against Apollodoros; or Andokides' nasty attack on Chrysilla, the wife of Ischomachos (who is also the virtuous wife in Xenophon's *Oikonomikos*, Harvey 1984), provide interesting examples of this. Again, although it could be argued that in the courtroom context men may be using women to attack other men (though this is hard to see in Apollodoros' case), the fact remains that women would most certainly have known of such accusations of themselves or other women, and hence their own, everyday relationships with other women (and men, for that matter) would have been affected by courtroom proceedings, regardless of the truth of the allegations or possibly even the outcome of the case. The ability of Archippe or Chrysilla to compete effectively with other women on their own behalf and for the sake of their households would have been jeopardized by unpleasant allegations in court (whether their names are mentioned or not is irrelevant to the fact that most of the audience will know who they are). And perhaps this was part of the intention of the accusers.

Third, and more difficult, is the extent to which laws (as supposedly impartial norms) designed to regulate the lives of women at a formal level actually operated at the level of everyday life. For the wealthy women for whom we have most evidence there are sometimes glaring disparities between legal formalities and lived realities. Hence, despite the fact that there was apparently a law that women could not dispose of more than the value of one medimnos of barley (Isaios 10. 10), Archippe ([Demosthenes] 45) owns and manages a *synoikia* (tenement house), the wife of Polyeuktos (Demosthenes 41) was in charge of many large-scale financial transactions, and Demosthenes' mother is said by Aphobos to have had control (*kyria*) of 4 talents in cash (Demosthenes 27. 53, 55; 28. 47–8). On the other hand, although there is no surviving law that prohibits women from owning land and real property in Athens, and I think there never was such a law (*contra* Schaps 1979, Cohen 1987, and others), it is clear that wealthy women usually owned moveable rather than real property, though a few instances of the latter are known (see Foxhall 1989; also a *horos* (an inscribed stone-marking property serving as security on a loan) that was probably securing a house owned by a woman, Finley 1985:192, no. 175A). In this case social preference was frequently stronger than legal right. Indeed, even in the question of citizenship, legal rules could be bent, when wealthy and influential men wished to register illegitimate children or children who were not their own on phratry and deme registers as citizens (e.g. Euktemon in Isaios 6. 21–5 registers an illegitimate son as a citizen, and makes a deal over the inheritance with his legitimate son so that the latter will not object; Stephanos in [Demosthenes] 59. 38 is alleged to have bragged that he could do this for the children of Neaira). Hence, although formal law clearly affected the way people lived their lives, and their relationships to others, it is also clear that in many circumstances laws were circumvented or ignored (as well as dubiously or even incorrectly cited and applied—e.g. Demosthenes 43, Isaios 10. 10), and many ambiguities in the status of relationships, persons, and property resulted.

Fourth, it is interesting how many disputes which become court battles between men seem to have begun as quarrels between, involving, or even generated by women. [Demosthenes] 45, mentioned above, is a case in point: Apollodoros' battle was at least as much with his mother as with Phormion, his opponent. Similarly in Demosthenes 41, the scenario is clearly one of two sisters (who have no brothers) fighting over the division of their patrimony through their husbands, in court. In fact, the younger of the two sisters, Kleiokrateia, who was married to the defendant in this case, seems to have been financially successful enough to dedicate in her own name a statue made by Praxiteles to Demeter and Kore (Shear 1937: 341).

In [Demosthenes] 55 the dispute at issue was whether a wall built by the speaker had blocked a seasonal watercourse and caused flooding of his neighbour's property when a heavy rainstorm occurred. The quarrel escalated into a lawsuit. But the real source of flame-fanning in this case is made clear at 55. 23–5, 27, where it is related that the defendant's mother visited the plaintiff's mother after the event, and the two women argued (the defendant's mother maintained the damage was trivial). The speaker (who is the defendant) challenges his opponent's mother to swear an oath that the damage was serious, for his mother is willing to swear that it was not (55. 27).

Indeed, oaths, or rather the offer of an oath, frequently constitute a means by which men 'involve' women in a court case and insert their testimony or alleged testimony (cf. Thür, this volume). It is interesting to speculate to what extent the impetus for such interjections came from the women themselves. Or did husbands simply invent what their female relations 'ought' to say, without consulting them? Surely both scenarios are equally likely and both must have occurred. But it is noteworthy that in the one case in which a woman is reported to have actually sworn an oath

(Demosthenes 39. 3–4) she apparently took matters into her own hands and betrayed the man on whose behalf she was swearing.

The best-documented dispute, with resulting court cases, which was incited by a woman is Demosthenes' recovery of his patrimony from his dishonest guardians (Demosthenes 27–30). However impressive we may think Demosthenes' rhetorical abilities for a young man, the real heroine of this social drama is his mother, Kleoboule. Her role in the events after the death of Demosthenes' father has been plausibly and perceptively analysed by Hunter (1989), and my reconstruction of those events differs from Hunter's only in minor details. Kleoboule had probably nagged and primed Demosthenes for years to take court action as soon as he came to manhood so as to vindicate her. Indeed, for the earlier events, Demosthenes was explicitly dependent on the information provided by his mother (Demosthenes 27. 40, 28. 26, 33), and on several occasions his evidence is supported by her readiness to swear oaths (29. 26, 33, 56).

Demosthenes' father (also named Demosthenes) had died when he was 7 and his sister was 5. His father made a will, which he validated on his deathbed, that his sister's son, Aphobos, was to marry his widow, Kleoboule, who brought with her a large dowry, and he was to have the house to live in until Demosthenes grew up. The elder Demosthenes' brother Demon's son, Demophon, was to marry his daughter (Demosthenes' sister) when she came of age, bringing with her an even larger dowry (though the prospective husband would get hold of the money immediately). These two nephews, Aphobos and Demophon, were with Demosthenes' father's friend, Therippides, to be joint guardians of the considerable property of his son (Demosthenes) until he reached maturity (see Fig. 5 for family relationships). After the elder Demosthenes' death, Aphobos moved into the house, got hold of Kleoboule's dowry, and started dealing with the household's resources in a way to which she strongly objected. By rights, Aphobos ought to have been her *kyrios*, but she clearly appealed to an alternative *kyrios*, Demochares, the husband of her sister Philia (Hunter 1989: 40). When Demochares queried Aphobos about his behaviour, the latter said he was just having a spot of bother with her over the jewellery (27.15), but it would all be sorted out. Shortly afterward, Aphobos moved out and kept hold of the dowry belonging to Demosthenes' mother, Kleoboule, for the next ten years, until Demosthenes came of age and prosecuted him

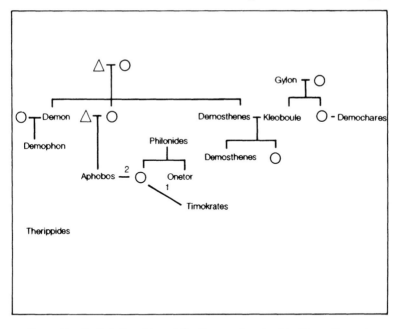

Fɪɢ. 5 Family Relationships of the Persons involved in Demosthenes'
Inheritance Dispute (Demosthenes 27–30)

for its return and for mismanagement of his estate. Demochares did
nothing (legally at least) to help his sister-in-law throughout this
period.

Demosthenes also alleged that Aphobos, Demophon, and
Therippides mismanaged his estate, and did not lease it out to the
highest bidder (ideally an impartial third party) as was 'normal'
practice for the estates of orphans in Athens, although it is notable,
and perhaps odd, that Aphobos was never prosecuted by any of the
potentially interested parties (such as Demochares) for this under
the legally available provision of the procedure known as *phasis*
(Harrison 1968: 115–17; MacDowell 1978: 94; Todd 1993: 41,
119). In addition, Aphobos remained unmarried until just before
Demosthenes reached manhood and full citizenship, whereupon he
married a woman who was already married, the wife of
Timokrates, daughter of Philonides of Melite and sister of Onetor.

Of course we do not have all the facts in this case, for only one side of the story survives. But the simplest explanation of some of these rather odd events is that the situation was not, as Demosthenes skilfully implied (but did not say outright), that Aphobos refused to marry his mother, but rather that his mother gave Aphobos the boot and refused to marry him.

Demosthenes' mother, Kleoboule, and her older sister, Philia, were the daughters of the eminent but notorious fifth-century BC general Gylon. Although Gylon seems to have spent much of his life outside Athens, his two daughters (who were *epikleroi*, i.e. girls with no living brothers or father) both married Athenian citizens and lived in Athens (Hunter 1989: 40). Kleoboule seems to have been a very tough lady. As I reconstruct events, when the elder Demosthenes died, his wife reckoned that the interests of her marital household, her children, and herself were not those of Aphobos. She refused to marry him and sent him away, but not before he had got hold of her dowry money. Why did Aphobos remain unmarried until just before Demosthenes reached maturity? Because that way he could claim it was all her fault. And also he could not easily be prosecuted for the return of the dowry, since, he could say, he was ready to marry her at any time—perhaps he even hoped to do so. But, just in case, he seems to have had a potential wife waiting in the wings, Onetor's sister, who had been married to Timokrates 'temporarily' until such time as Aphobos might claim her. Had Aphobos actually managed to marry Kleoboule, Onetor's sister would at least have had a husband, though perhaps one not quite so rich or prestigious as Aphobos. Significantly, she was married to Aphobos directly from the house of Timokrates, who was apparently a willing party to the arrangement (Demosthenes 30. 11). And, according to Demosthenes (30. 7 ff.), Timokrates kept the principal of her dowry and paid a special discount rate of interest to Aphobos. This was presumably not, as Demosthenes accuses, because Onetor did not trust Aphobos with the dowry (30. 10), but because the whole thing was a scheme cooked up by Onetor and Aphobos, with the compliance (for remuneration) of Timokrates. Aphobos only seems to have married this woman when he no longer had any hope of marrying Kleoboule, the mother of Demosthenes.

Similarly, Aphobos managed not to lease out the estate (Demosthenes seems to reckon this is largely Aphobos' fault), or to be prosecuted for this omission. Had he married the widow and become Demosthenes' stepfather it would not have been expected that he lease out the estate, since now he would have been part of the household (see, for example, Isaios 9. 28-9, where it seems to be assumed as normal that a stepfather should manage his stepson's patrimonial estate). If Kleoboule had appealed to her brother-in-law, Demochares, as an 'alternative' *kyrios*, to take legal or some other kind of action on her behalf, there is probably little that he could have done for her or her household even if he had been willing, if the situation were that *she* refused the marriage on offer. This may also explain why she was never married to anyone else, for the family was still quite wealthy, despite the alleged 'theft' of the dowry and other property. And Demosthenes' statement that his mother voluntarily took on a life of widowhood for the sake of her children (28. 26) is probably also explained by her refusal to marry Aphobos.

That Kleoboule remained in economic control of the household for these ten years is quite clear, as she was able to supply Demosthenes with detailed accounts of the family enterprises over this period (cf. Hunter 1989: 43-6). It is also suggested by Aphobos' accusation, repudiated by Demosthenes (Demosthenes 27. 53, 55; 28. 47-8), that she was managing 4 talents handed over to her by the elder Demosthenes.

It is interesting to compare the story of Demosthenes' fatherless household with that of the orphans in Lysias 32. It is difficult to be sure of all the details here, since the speech is incomplete. But the similarity of some of the circumstances emphasizes the significance of the differences between the two cases. Diogeiton and Diodotos were brothers who, on the death of their father, divided the moveable property but not the real estate (see Fig. 6). Diogeiton had an only daughter, and since his brother had done well in shipping with his share of the inheritance, he encouraged her marriage to Diodotos. This couple had three children, two sons and a daughter. When Diodotos went off to fight in the Peloponnesian War, as was customary he made a will and arranged his affairs in the event of his death. Allegedly, he left 5 talents and other assets in the charge of Diogeiton, as well as 7 talents 40 minas in outstanding bottomry loans (his children's patrimony, for Diogeiton was their guardian). He also left a dowry, a trousseau ('the contents of the room'), and a separate cash inheritance for his wife, and a dowry for his daughter (the speaker is the husband of this daughter) (Lysias 32. 4-8).

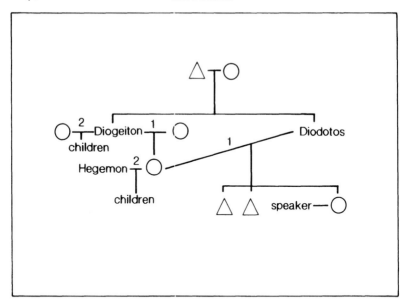

FIG. 6 Family Relationships of the Persons involved in Lysias 32

Diodotos was killed in battle at Ephesos. After his death, his wife was married off to Hegemon, supposedly having accepted a lower dowry than she had been bequeathed (32. 8). Subsequently children were born of this union (32. 13). The elder of the two sons of Diodotos and Diogeiton's daughter did not attain his majority until 8 years after his father's death, and when he did he was told that none of his father's money remained (32. 9). For a year or so after their father died these children had lived with Diogeiton, then they were moved out to another house (32. 8, 16). It would be interesting to know whether this coincided with the remarriage of Diogeiton, a union which also produced offspring (32. 17). When the elder son came of age and was thus entitled to claim his inheritance, Diogeiton informed him and his younger brother that their patrimony had been legitimately spent on their maintenence. The two brothers then rallied their brother-in-law, the speaker, to their support—it is possible the two brothers were even living with the speaker and their sister (though this is speculation).

The interesting difference from Demosthenes' case is the behaviour of the mother (Diogeiton's daughter), and the contrast between that behaviour and the image of it promoted by her son-in-law, the speaker. Kleoboule, Demosthenes' mother, in actuality retained the position of head of her late husband's household, despite all attempts to dislodge her from it. Diogeiton's daughter, in contrast, forfeited any authority she might have been able to claim to her father. The fact that she was fobbed off with a smaller dowry than that to which she was entitled suggests either that the speaker is lying (which is perfectly possible) or, perhaps more likely, that she had neither the courage nor the wits, nor perhaps the resources of Kleoboule, and simply submitted to her father.

None the less, her supposedly courageous defiance against this unjust authority (a fabrication in my opinion) was central to the case of the children. According to the speaker, Diogeiton's daughter was appealed to by her eldest son by Diodotos, and the sons and their mother entreated the speaker for assistance. But it was the speaker who organized the gathering of relatives (including her second husband, Hegemon) at which Diogeiton's daughter allegedly made her stirring speech, brought forward proofs that her children by her first marriage had been defrauded, and offered to uphold them by oath. The account of this meeting makes it sound very staged, almost as if she had been given a script by the children of her first marriage and her son-in-law. The unfortunate reality for these children was, I think, that after the remarriage of their mother and their grandfather/uncle, and the birth of children to both of these unions, no one with any serious political persona (except the man married to the daughter of Diodotos) had any interest in the integrity of the natal household of Diodotos' children, and they were effectively surplus to the households to which they were most closely related. Here it would seem that these children suffered precisely because their mother was *not* strong-minded and independent like Kleoboule, but instead conformed to the male ideal of female submissiveness.

## 4. GUARDIANSHIP: WOMEN AND LEGAL AUTHORITY

These complicated cases bring up two other aspects of women's involvement in and manipulation of legal institutions. The first is the issue of *kyrieia*, 'guardianship', the second is the issue of women as the victims of male machinations. The surviving lawcourt

speeches suggest that *kyrieia* is a much fuzzier, less formalized institution than social and legal historians have generally thought
(compare also the excellent discussion of the notion of *kyrieia* in
relation to women in Hunter 1989: 43–7). Women often had several potential *kyrioi* and could sometimes play one off against
another—this is what Demosthenes' mother clearly attempted to
do. Moreover, some *kyrioi* were more likely to work enthusiastically
for the greatest benefit of a woman than others, depending in large
part on their relationship to her and to other women. The *kyrios*
over whom a mother is most likely to have had most influence and
thus control was an adult son. However, once he was married, a
mother's interests might have to compete with those of a wife. It
was probably the case that the more distant the kinship relationship, the less incentive a *kyrios* had to work to a woman's advantage, and the more competing interests (often from other women)
he might also have. It was probably also generally the case that the
more potential closely related *kyrioi* were available to a woman
(and the more powerful they were), the better were her chances of
holding her own when difficulties arose. For example, in Isaios 6
the elderly Euktemon probably had divorced his wife. She exercised
her right to remain in the marital home with her adult sons, and
seems to have made life so unpleasant for Euktemon that he went
to live in a brothel that he owned. In contrast, Demosthenes begs
the jury that his mother should not be robbed of her remaining
hopes (28. 20). *He*, as her newly adult son, with her interests at
heart, personifies them (cf. Hunter 1989: 46–7). The malleable and
manipulable nature of *kyrieia* as an institution also makes it difficult
to argue that female identities were in any real sense derivative
from it, or that women's identities were any more tied to family
than men's (though it is certainly true that the relation of identity
to family was different for women than for men).

　　The other side of *kyrieia* is that women could indeed become victims of men's plots, and if they were not as fierce as Archippe or
Demosthenes' mother, and if they had no alternative *kyrioi*, they
might well be exploited. For example, in Isaios 3 the two claimants
to the disputed inheritance are both women. Naturally they are
represented in court by men who are (or claim to be) closely related
to them. Because of the degree of potential misrepresentation of
these women, it is almost impossible to judge the merits of either
side in this complex case. None the less, it looks as though either

at least one of the women has been cheated by a conspiracy of the men related to her, or she is being illicitly exploited by a male associate. Similarly in Isaios 10. 18 a woman allegedly asked her husband to pursue her claim to an estate as an *epikleros*, but he desisted when her agnatic relatives threatened to claim her themselves and remove her from her husband.

Sometimes, too, women seem to be blamed when men do not wish to take responsibility for actions and events, or involve other men in uncomfortable affairs. In Lysias 1, although the plaintiff (if he is telling the truth) is legally in the right, in terms of the prevailing social ethos of competition he is in the wrong, for he has been out-competed by the adulterer. Hence perhaps the need to stress that the reason he had not found out about his wife's affair sooner was because it was communicated through female channels. Significantly, it is another woman with whom Eratosthenes is having an affair who reveals the illicit intrigues of the speaker's wife (1. 15). And (supposedly) part of the speaker's wife's seduction by Eratosthenes includes attending the Thesmophoria with Eratosthenes' mother (1. 20)! Whether it was true or not, the plausibility of a network of women conspiring against men was clearly real in the minds of men.

In [Demosthenes] 48 the speaker and his wife's brother colluded in claiming an inheritance which had many claimants. This court case arose because they had quarrelled with each other, and the reason given for the quarrel is that the *hetaira*, 'courtesan', with whom the wife's brother lived did not get on with the speaker's wife (the opponent's sister) and daughters. It is impossible to determine the truth, but this could easily be a way of shifting responsibility for a family disagreement onto the women. Interestingly, although the speaker says his brother-in-law lives with a *hetaira* he does not mention her name, so this too may be a slanderous attack on a legitimate wife, which would surely have repercussions outside the court. One of the best (or rather, worst) examples of victimized women is that of the wicked stepmother and the dumped courtesan of Antiphon 1 (another case of women allegedly conspiring against men). These are women who have been rejected by their men, but whose reaction is anything but passive, even judging from what is likely to be a highly distorted version of events.

In conclusion, it is clear that women's lives and women's actions were not separated from the male world of lawcourts but lived in continuum with it, as they were construed by it. Women acted upon and were aware of events that happened here, and themselves acted on their menfolk to influence the outcome of events in this arena (cf. [Demosthenes] 59. 110-11; Isaios 12. 5). Obviously they were frequently successful in this aim. Undoubtedly many women were victims of a system that was heavily male-dominated, but they were not passive victims. Many were strong women who spent their lives fighting for themselves and their families, in the continual but shifting conflict between households that made up Athenian life. Athenian men and women used law to compete, to mediate and shape relationships and non-relationships which were also acted out in other contexts. Of course law was used to this end differently by men than by women, as it also affected men and women differently. But for both men and women, law had more to do with alliance, prestige, and conflict than it did with social order and dispute settlement. In short, law in classical Athens lived not only in the courts and the agora and the places of men, but made its way through the quiet back streets and the fountain houses where women walked.

# List of Contributors

JOHN K. DAVIES is Professor of Ancient History at the University of Liverpool, and author of *Athenian Propertied Families* (Oxford, 1971), *Wealth and the Power of Wealth in Classical Athens and* (New York, 1979), and, with R. A. Reid, *Demosthenes: Selected Private Speeches* (1985) for Cambridge and Latin Classics.

MARGARETHA DEBRUNNER HALL lectures at University College London. She is the author of *Autorität und Kontinuität: Studien zur athenischen Demokratie des 4. Jahrhundert* (1995).

LIN FOXHALL is Lecturer in Ancient History at the School of Archaeoogical Studies, University of Leicester. She has written *Olive Cultivation in Ancient Greece: The Ancient Economy Revisited* (London, 1996), and will shortly publish *Studying Gender in Classical Antiquity* (Cambridge) and *When Men were Men: Masculinity, Power and Identity in Classical Antiquity* (Routledge)

ANDREW LEWIS is Senior Lecturer in Laws at University College London. He has published numerous articles on many aspects of legal history and is the co-editor, with D. J. Ibbetson, of *The Roman Law Tradition* (Cambridge, 1994).

TREVOR SAUNDERS is Professor of Greek at the University of Newcastle-Upon-Tyne. He is the author of *Plato's Penal Code: Tradition, Controversy and Reform in Greek Penology* (Oxford, 1991).

ROSALIND THOMAS is Lecturer in Classics and History at Royal Holloway, University of London. She is the author of *Oral Tradition and Written Record in Classical Athens* (Cambridge, 1989) and *Literacy and Orality in Ancient Greece* (Cambridge, 1992).

STEPHEN TODD is Lecturer in Classics at the University of Keele. He is the co-cditor of *Nomos: Essays in Athenian Law* (Oxford, 1993).

GERHARD THÜR is Professor of Roman Law at Karl-Franzens-Universität Graz, Austria. He specializes in Greek and Hellenistic legal history. He is the author of *Beweisführung vor den Schwurgerichtshöfen Athens: Die proklesis zur basanos* (Vienna 1977) and, with H. Taeuber, *Prozessrechtliche Inschriften der griechischen Poleis: Arkadien* (Vienna, 1994). Since 1985 he has edited numerous volumes of *Symposion : Akten der Gesellschaft für Griechische und Hellenistische Rechtsgeschiechte.*

# List of References

ALBINI, U. (1952), 'Lysia narratore', *Maia*, 5: 182-90.

ANDERSEN, Ø. (1989), 'The Significance of Writing in Early Greece-A Critical Appraisal', in K. Schousboe and M. T. Larson (eds.), *Literacy and Society*. (Copenhagen), 73-90.

BEKKER, I. (1965) (ed.), *Anecdota Graeca*. i. *Lexica Sequerina* (Graz; 1st pub. 1814-21).

BERNEKER, E. (1968) (ed.), *Zur griechischen Rechtsgeschichte*, Wege der Forschung 45 (Darmstadt).

—— (1971), 'Der Felssturz im alten griechischen Recht', in *Studi in onore di E. Volterra*, vol. 1. (Milan), 87-97.

BILE, M. (1988), *Le Dialecte crétois ancienne* (Paris).

BLASS, F. (1887), *Die attische Beredsamkeit*, vol. 1, 2nd edn. (Leipzig).

BOARDMAN, J. (1970), 'Orientalen auf Kreta', in *Dädalische Kunst auf Kreta im 7. Jahrhundert v. Chr.*, for the 80th birthday of F. Matz, Hamburg Museum (Mainz), 14-25.

—— (1980), *The Greeks Overseas*, 2nd edn. (London).

BÖCKH, A. (1886), *Die Staatshaushaltung der Athener*, 3rd edn. (Leipzig).

BOEGEHOLD, A. L. (1972), 'The Establishment of a Central Archive at Athens', *American Journal of Archaeology*, 76: 23-30.

—— (1990), 'Andokides and the Decree of Patrokleides', *Historia*, 39: 149-62.

BONNER, R. (1973), 'The Use of Hemlock for Capital Punishment', in *Athenian Studies presented to William Scott Ferguson, Harvard Studies in Classical Philology*, suppl. 1 (Cambridge, Mass.).

—— and SMITH G. (1930, 1938), *The Administration of Justice from Homer to Aristotle*, vols. 1 & 2. (Chicago).

BOTTÉRO, J. (1982), 'Le 'Code' de Hammu-rabi', *Annali della Scuola Normale Superiore di Pisa*, 12: 409-44.

BOURDIEU, P. (1977), *Outline of a Theory of Practice* (Cambridge).

—— (1990), *The Logic of Practice* (Cambridge).

BUCK, C. D. (1955), *The Greek Dialects* (Chicago).

BURDON, J. (1988), 'Slavery as a Punishment in Roman Criminal Law', in L. Archer (ed.), *Slavery and Other Forms of Unfree Labour* (London), 68-85.

156     Bibliography

BUSOLT, G. (1920), *Griechische Staatskunde* in I. Müller (series ed.), *Handbuch der Altertumswissenschaft*, vol. 4. 1. 1. (Munich).

CAMASSA, G. (1988), 'Aux origines de la codification écrite des lois en Grèce', in Detienne (1988a), 130-55.

CANTARELLA, E. (1984), 'Per una preistoria del castigo', in *Du châtiment dans la cité: Supplices corporels et peine de mort dans le monde antique*, Collection de l'École française de Rome 79 (Rome), 37-73.

—— (1987), 'In fondo al barathron', in *Studi A. Biscardi, vol. 4* (Milan), 493-506.

—— (1988), 'La lapidazione tra rito, vendetta e diritto', in M. M. Mactoux and E. Geny (eds.), *Mélanges Pierre Lévêque*, vol. 1. (Paris), 83-95.

—— (1991), 'Moicheia: Reconsidering a Problem', in M. Gagarin (ed.), *Symposion 1990: Papers on Greek and Hellenistic Legal History* (Cologne), 289-96.

CARTER, L. B. (1986), *The Quiet Athenian* (Oxford).

CARTLEDGE, P., MILLETT P., and TODD S., (1990) (eds.), *Nomos: Essays in Athenian Law, Politics and Society* (Cambridge).

CATAUDELLA, M. R. (1973), 'L'interpretazione delle parole ἀκεύοντος e il ruolo del tutore nel codice di Gortyna, col. II. 17-20', *Rendiconti Istituto Lombardo, Classe di Lettere, Scienze morale e storiche*, 107: 799-809.

CERRI, G. (1979), *Legislazione orale e tragedia greca: Studi sull'Antigone di Sofocle e sulle Supplici di Euripide* (Naples).

CHARPIN, D. (1986), *Le Clergé d'Ur au siècle d'Hammurabi* (Geneva).

CLINTON, K. (1982), 'The Nature of the Late Fifth-Century revision of the Athenian Law Code', *Hesperia* suppl., 19: 27-37.

COHEN, D. (1983a), *Theft in Athenian Law* (Munich).

—— (1983b), 'The Athenian Law of Adultery', *Revue Internationale des Droits de l'Antiquite*, 31: 147-65.

—— (1987), 'The Legal Status and Political Role of Women in Plato's Laws', *Revue Internationale des Droits de l'Antiquité*, 34: 27-40.

—— (1991), *Law, Sexuality and Society* (Cambridge).

COLLINS, WILKIE (1876), *The Law and the Lady* (London).

COLLITZ, H. (1884-1915) (ed.), *Sammlung der griechischen Dialekt-Inschriften*, vols. 1-4 (Göttingen).

CONNOR, W. R. (1988), ' "Sacred" and "Secular": Ἱερὰ καὶ ὅσια and the Classical Athenian Concept of the State', *Ancient Society*, 19: 161-88.

DEBRUNNER, M. K. (1988), 'Das zweigliedrige "Strafrecht" des Aristotles: Geschlagene Amtsträger und unfreiwillige Rechtsbeziehungen, *Zeitschrift Savigny-stiftung für Rechtsgeshichte (romisches Abteilung)* 105: 680-94.

DE STE CROIX, G. E. M. (1981), *Class Struggle in the Ancient Greek World* (London).

DERENNE, E. (1930), *Les procès d'impiété intentè aux philosophes à Athenès au Vᵐe et au IVᵐe siècles avant J.-C.* (Liège).

DETIENNE, M. (1988a), *Les Savoirs de l'écriture en Grèce ancienne*, Cahiers de Philologie 14 (Lille).

—— (1988b), 'L'Espace de la publicité: Ses operateurs intellectuels dans la cité', in Detienne (1988a) 29-81.

DIELS, H., and KRANZ W., (1951-2), *Die Fragmente der Vorsokratiker*, 3 vols. 6th edn. (Berlin).

DOVER, K. J. (1968), *Lysias and the Corpus Lysiacum* (Berkeley).

—— (1978), *The Greeks and their Legacy* (Oxford), 135-58 (1st pub. 1976 as 'The Freedom of the Intellectual in Greek Society', *Talanta*, 7: 24-54).

—— Dow, S. (1955-7), 'The Law Codes of Athens', *Proceedings of the Massachusetts Historical Society*, 71: 3-37.

—— (1960), 'The Athenian Calendar of Sacrifices: The Chronology of Nikomakhos' Second Term', *Historia*, 9: 270-93.

—— (1961), 'The Walls Inscribed with Nikomakhos' Law Code', *Hesperia*, 30: 58-73.

DUCREY, P. (1971), 'Note sur le crucifixion', *Museun Helveticum*, 28: 183-5.

EDER, W. (1986), 'The Political Significance of the Codification of Law in Archaic Societies: An Unconventional Hypothesis', in K. Raaflaub (ed.), *Social Struggles in Archaic Rome* (Berkeley), 262-300.

EDWARDS, G. P., and EDWARDS, R. B., (1974), 'Red Letters and Phoenician Writing', *Kadmos*, 13: 48-57.

—— (1977), 'The Meaning and Etymology of *ΠΟΙΝΙΚΑΣΤΑΣ*', *Kadmos*, 16: 131-40.

VAN EFFENTERRE, H. (1973), 'Le Contrat de travail du scribe Spensithios', *Bulletin de Correspondance Hellenique*, 97: 31-46.

—— and VAN EFFENTERRE, M. (1994), 'Arbitrages homeriques', ed. G. Thür, *Symposion 1993. Vorträge der griechischen und hellenistischen Rechtsgeschichte* (Cologne), 3-15.

ENGELMANN, H., and MERKELBACH, R., (1972) (eds.), *Inschriften von Erythrai in Klazomenai* (Bonn).

FAHR, W. (1969), Θεοὺς νομίζειν: *Zum Problem der Anfänge des Atheismus bei den Griechen* (Hildesheim).

FINGARETTE, A. (1971), 'A New Look at the Wall of Nikomakhos', *Hesperia*, 40: 330-5.

FINKELSTEIN, J. J. (1961), 'Ammi-Saduqa's Edict and the Babylonian "Law Codes" ', *Journal of Cuneiform Studies*, 15: 91-104.

FINLEY, M. I. (1985), *Studies in Land and Credit in Ancient Athens, 500-200 BC: The Horos Inscriptions*, Introduction by P.Millet (New Brunswick, NJ; 1st pub. 1952).

—— (1983), *Politics in the Ancient World* (Cambridge).

—— (1986), *The Use and Abuse of History*, 2nd edn. (London).

FISHER, N. R. E. (1990), 'The Law of *Hubris* in Athens', in Cartledge *et al.* (1990) 123-38.

FISHER, N. R. E. (1992), *Hybris: a Study in the Values of Honour and Shame in Ancient Greece* (Warminster).

FOUCAULT, M. (1977), *Discipline and Punish: The Birth of the Prison*, trans. Alan Sheridan (Harmondsworth).

FOXHALL, L. (1989), 'Household, Gender and Property in Classical Athens', *Classical Quarterly*, 39: 22-44.

—— (1990), 'Olive Cultivation within Greek and Roman Agriculture: the Ancient Economy Revisited,' Ph.D. thesis. (Liverpool).

—— (1991), 'Response to Eva Cantarella', in M. Gagarin (ed.), *Symposion 1990: Papers on Greek and Hellenistic Legal History* (Cologne), 297-304.

FRANCKEN, C. M. (1865), *Commentationes Lysiacae* (Utrecht).

GAGARIN, M. (1981), *Drakon and Early Athenian Homicide Law* (New Haven).

—— (1982), 'The Organization of the Gortyn Law Code', *Greek, Roman and Byzantine Studies*, 23: 129-46.

—— (1984), 'The Testimony of Witnesses in the Gortyn Laws', *Greek, Roman and Byzantine Studies*, 25: 345-9.

—— (1986), *Early Greek Law* (Berkeley).

—— (1988), 'The First Law of the Gortyn Code', *Greek, Roman and Byzantine Studies*, 29: 335-43.

GEERTZ, C. (1983), 'Local Knowledge: Fact and Law in Comparative Perspective', in *Local Knowledge: Further Essays in Interpretive Anthropology* (New York), 167-234.

GERNET, L. (1916), 'Observations sur la loi de Gortyne', *Revue des études grecques*, 29: 383-408 (Rev. in Gernet (1955).

—— (1955), *Droit et société dans la Grèce ancienne.* (Paris).

—— (1976), *Anthropologie de la Grèce antique* (Paris); Eng. trans. as *The Anthropology of Ancient Greece*, trans. J. Hamilton and B. Nagy (Baltimore 1981).

—— (1981a), 'Capital Punishment', in *The Anthropology of Ancient Greece* (Baltimore), 252-76 (1st pub. 1924 as 'Sur l'exécution capitale', *Revue des études grecques*, 37: 261-93).

—— (1981b), 'Some Connections between Punishment and Religion', in *The Anthropology of Ancient Greece* (Baltimore), 240-51 (1st pub. 1936 as 'Quelques rapports entre la pénalité et la religion dans la Grèce ancienne', *Antiquité classique*, 5: 325-9).

—— and BIZOS, M. (1955), *Lysias: Discours*, 2 vols., 3rd edn. (Budé edn., Paris).

GOMME, A. W., ANDREWES, A., and DOVER, K. J. (1981), *A Historical Commentary on Thucydides*, vol. 5 (Oxford).

GOODY, J. (1986), *The Logic of Writing and the Organization of Society* (Cambridge).

—— and WATT, I., (1968), 'The Consequences of Literacy', in J. Goody (ed.), *Literacy in Traditional Societies* (Cambridge), 27-68.

GRAS, M. (1984), 'Cité grecque et lapidation', in *Du châtiment dans la cité: Supplices corporels et peine de mort dans le monde antique*, Collection de l'École française de Rome, 79 (Rome), 75-89.

GUARDUCCI, M. (1950), *Inscriptione Creticae, IV: Tituli Gortynii* (Rome).

GÜLDE, O. (1882), *Quaestiones de Lysiae oratione in Nicomachum* (Berlin).

GUTHRIE, W. K. C. (1971), *The Sophists* (Cambridge).

HAINSWORTH, J. B. (1972) (ed.), *Tituli ad dialectos Graecas illustrandas selecti*, vol.2. (Leiden).

HANSEN, M. H. (1975), *Eisangelia, the Sovereignty of the People's Court in Athens in the Fourth Century B.C. and the Impeachment of Generals and Politicians* (Odense).

—— (1976), *Apagoge, Endeixis and Ephegesis against Kakourgoi, Atimoi and Pheugontes: A Study in the Athenian Administration of Justice in the Fourth Century B.C.* (Odense).

—— (1978), '*Nomos* and *psephisma* in Fourth-Century Athens', *Greek, Roman and Byzantine Studies*,19: 315-30.

—— (1980), 'Athenian *nomothesia* in the Fourth Century B.C. and Demosthenes' Speech against Leptines', *Classica et mediaevalia*, 32: 87-104.

—— (1983), *The Athenian Ecclesia: A Collection of Articles, 1976-1983* (Copenhagen).

—— (1985), 'Athenian *nomothesia*', *Greek, Roman and Byzantine Studies*, 26: 345-71.

—— (1990), 'Diokles' Law (Demosthenes XIV.42) and the Revision of the Athenian Corpus of Laws in the Archonship of Eukleides', *Classica et mediaevalia*, 41: 63-71.

HARDING, C., and IRELAND, R.W., (1989), *Punishment: Rhetoric, Rule and Practice* (London).

HARRIS, E. (1990), 'Did the Athenians Regard Seduction as a Worse Crime than Rape?', *Classical Quarterly*, 40: 370-7.

—— (1994), 'Law and Oratory', in Worthington (1994), 130-150.

HARRIS, W. V. (1989), *Ancient Literacy* (Cambridge, Mass.).

HARRISON, A. R. W. (1955), 'Law-Making at Athens at the End of the Fifth Century B.C.', *Journal of Hellenic Studies*, 75: 26-35.

—— (1968), *The Law of Athens*, vol.1: *The Family and Property* (Oxford).

—— (1971), *The Law of Athens*, vol.2: *Procedure* (Oxford).

HART, H. L. A. (1961), *The Concept of Law* (Oxford; 2nd edn. 1995).

HARVEY, F. D. (1984), 'The Wicked Wife of Ischomachos', *Échos du Monde Classique/Classical Views*, 28/1 (NS 3/1): 68-70.

HEADLAM, J. W. (1893), 'The Procedure of the Gortynian Inscription', *Journal of Hellenic Studies*, 13: 48-69.

HENGEL, M. (1977), *Crucifixion in the Ancient World and the Folly of the Cross* (London).

HENSE, O. (1911–12) (ed.), Stobaeus, *Anthologii libri duo posteriores* (Berlin).

HERDT, G. (1987), *The Sambia. Ritual and Gender in New Guinea.* (New York).

HERRMANN, P. (1981), 'Teos und Abdera im 5. Jahrhundert v. Chr.', *Chiron*, 11: 1–30.

HILLGRUBER, M. (1988), *Die zehnte Rede des Lysias: Einleitung, Text und Kommentar* (Berlin).

HIRZEL, R. (1900), *Agraphos nomos*, Abhandlungen der Sächsischen Akademie der Wissenschaften, Philologische-Historischen Klasse, 1903, no. 1 (Leipzig).

HOMMEL, H. (1928), Review of A. Steinwenter, *Die Streitbendigung durch Urteil, Schiedsspruch und Vergleich nach greichischen Rechte*, in *Philologische Wochenschrift*, 48: 359–68.

—— (1969), 'Die Gerichtsszene auf dem Schild des Achilleus: Zur Pflege des Rechts in homerischer Zeit', in P. Steinmetz (ed.), *Politeia und Res Publica: Beiträge zum Verständnis von Politik, Recht und Stadt in der Antike dem Andenken*, Rudolf Starks gewidmet Palingenesia, vol.4 (Wiesbaden), 11–38.

HUMPHREYS, S. C. (1983), 'The Evolution of Legal Process in Ancient Attica', in E. Gabba (ed.), *Tria Corda (Festschrift Momigliano)* (Como), 229–56.

—— (1985), 'Law as Discourse', *History and Anthropology* 1: 241–64.

—— (1987), 'Law, Custom and Culture in Herodotus', *Arethusa*, 20: 211–20.

—— (1988), 'The Discourse of Law in Archaic and Classical Greece', *Law and History Review*, 6: 465–93.

HUNTER, V. (1989), 'Women's Authority in Classical Athens', *Échos du Monde Classique/Classical Views*, 8/1: 39–48.

—— (1994), *Policing Athens: Social Control in the Attic Lawsuits* (Princeton).

JEFFERY, L. H. (1990), *Local Scripts of Archaic Greece*, 2nd edn., supplement by A. Johnston (Oxford) (1st pub. 1961).

—— 1967: 'Ἀρχαῖα γράμματα: some ancient Greek views', in W. C. Brice (ed.), *Europa, Studien zur Geschichte und Epigraphik der frühen Aegaeis: Festschrift für E. Grumach* (Berlin) 152–66.

—— and MORPURGO-DAVIES A., (1970), '*ΠΟΙΝΙΚΑΣΤΑΣ* and *ΠΟΙΝΙΚΑΖΕΙΝ*: A New Archaic Inscription from Crete', *Kadmos*, 9: 118–54.

JENSEN, M. S. (1980), *The Homeric Question and the Oral-Formulaic Theory* (Copenhagen).

JONES, J. W. (1956), *The Law and Legal Theory of the Greeks* (Oxford).

JUST, R. (1989), *Women in Athenian Law and Life* (London).

KAHRSTEDT, U. (1938), 'Untersuchungen zu athenischen Behörden', *Klio*, 31: 1–32.

KEYSER, P. (1987), 'Numerals on the Gortynian Law-Codes (*IC* IV 72 and 73)', *Zeitschrift für Papyrologie und Epigraphik*, 69: 283–90.

KIESSLING, E. (1932), 'Mnemones', cols. 2261–4 in Pauly–Wissowa, (1940) *Real-Encyclopädie der classischen Altertumswissenschaft* (Stuttgart).

KLAFFENBACH, G. (1954), *Die Astynomeninschrift von Pergamon* (Berlin).

KOHLER, J., and ZIEBARTH, E., (1912), *Das Stadtrecht von Gortyn und seine Beziehungen zum gemeingrechischen Rechte* (Göttingen, repr. 1979, New York).

KOROŠEC, V. (1957), 'Le Problème de la codification dans le domaine du droit hittite', *Revue internationale des droits de l'antiquité*, 4: 93-105.

KRÄNZLEIN, A. (1963), *Eigentum und Besitz im griechischen Recht des 5. und 4. Jahrhundert v. Chr.* (Berlin).

KRAUS, F. R. (1960), 'Ein zentrales Problem des altmesopotamischen Rechts: Was ist der Codex Hammu-rabi?', *Genava²*, 8: 283-96.

KUNKEL, W. (1962), *Untersuchungen zur Entwicklung des römischen Kriminalverfahrens in vorsullanischer Zeit* (Munich).

LAMB, W. R. M. (1930), *Lysias* (Loeb Classical Library London).

LAMBRINUDAKIS, W., and WÖRRLE, M., (1983), 'Ein hellenistisches Reformgesetz über das öffentliche Urkunden wesen von Paros', *Chiron*, 13: 283-368.

LANGDON, M. K. (1976), *A Sanctuary of Zeus on Mt. Hymettus, Hesperia*, suppl.16.

LARSEN, J. A. O. (1949), 'The Origin and Significance of Counting Votes', *Classical Philology*, 44: 164-81.

LATTE, K. (1964), *Heiliges Recht. Untersuchungen zur Geschichte der sakralen Rechtsformen in Griechenland*, (Tübingen; 1st pub. 1920).

—— (1968a), 'Beiträge zum griechischen Strafrecht', in Berneker (1968), 263-311 (1st pub. 1931; also repr. in Latte (1968c)).

—— (1968a), 'Todesstrafe', in Latte (1968c), 393-415 (1st pub. Pauly-Wissowa (1940), *Real-Encyclopädie der classischen Altertumswissenschaft*, suppl. 7, s.v. 'Todesstrafe' (Stuttgart)).

—— (1968c), *Kleine Schriften* (Munich).

Laurencic, M. (1988), 'Ἀνδρεῖον'', *Tyche*, 3: 147-61.

LEMOSSE, M. (1957), 'Les Lois de Gortyne et la notion de codification', *Revue internationale des droits de l'antiquité*, 4: 131-7.

LEWIS, D. M. (1982), 'On the New Text of Teos', *Zeitschrift für Papyrologie und Epigraphik*, 47: 71-2.

—— (1990), 'The Political Background of Democritus', in E. M. Craik (ed.), *Owls to Athens. Essays on Classical Subjects Presented to Sir K. Dover* (Oxford), 151-4.

LEWIS, A. D. E., and IBBETSON, D. J., (1994) (eds.), *The Roman Law Tradition* (Cambridge).

LIPSIUS, J. (1905-15), *Das attische Recht* (Leipzig).

LOENING, R. (1903), *Geschichte der strafrechtlichen Zurechnungslehre* vol.1: *Die Zurechnungslehre des Aristoteles* (Jena).

LOENING, T. C. (1987), *The Reconciliation Agreement of 403/402 B.C. in Athens: Its Content and Application*, Hermes Einzelschrift, 53. (Stuttgart).

LORAUX, N. (1984), 'Le Corps étranglé', in *Du châtiment dans la cité: Supplices corporels et peine de mort dans le monde antique* Collection de l'École française de Rome, 79 (Rome), 195-224.

MacDowell, D. M. (1962), *Andokides On the Mysteries, the Text edited with Introduction, Commentary and Appendices* (Oxford).

—— (1975), 'Law-Making at Athens in the Fourth Century B.C.', *Journal of Hellenic Studies*, 95: 62-74.

—— (1978), *The Law in Classical Athens* (London).

MACKENZIE, M. M. (1981), *Plato on Punishment* (London).

MASCHKE, R. (1926), *Die Willenslehre in griechischen Recht* (Berlin).

MEIGGS, R., and LEWIS, D., (1988), *A Selection of Greek Historical Inscriptions to the End of the Fifth Century B.C.*, 2nd edn. (Oxford).

MERKELBACH, R. (1982), 'Zu dem neuen Text aus Teos', *Zeitschrift für Papyrologie und Epigraphik*, 46: 212-13.

MEYER-LAURIN, H. (1969), review of Willetts (1967), *Gnomon*, 41: 160-5.

MITSOS, M. T. (1983), 'Une inscription d'Argos', *Bulletin de Correspondance Hellénique*, 107: 243-9.

MITTEIS, L. (1891), *Reichrecht und Volksrecht in den östlichen Provinzen des römischen Kaiserreichs* (Leipzig).

MORROW, G. R. (1960), *Plato's Cretan City* (Princeton).

MÜHL, M. (1929), 'Die Gesetze des Zaleukos und Charondas', *Klio*, 22: 105-24; 432-63.

OLIVER, J., and DOW, S., (1935), 'Greek Inscriptions', *Hesperia*, 4: 1-107.

OSBORNE, R. (1985), 'Law in Action in Classical Athens', *Journal of Hellenic Studies*, 105: 40-58.

OSTWALD, M. (1969), *Nomos and the Beginnings of the Athenian Democracy* (Oxford).

—— (1973), 'Was There a Concept ἄγραφος νόμος in Classical Greece?', in E. N. Lee, A. P. D. Mourelatos, and R. M. Rorty (eds.), *Exegesis and Argument: Studies in Greek Philosophy presented to G. Vlastos, Phronesis* suppl. 1 (Assen), 70-104.

—— (1986), *From Popular Sovereignty to the Sovereignty of Law* (Berkeley).

PICCIRILLI, L. (1981), 'Nomoi cantati e nomoi scritti', *Civiltà classica e cristiana*, 2: 7-14.

RAUBITSCHEK, A. (1970), 'Supplementary Note', to Jeffery and Morpurgo-Davies (1970), *Kadmos*, 9: 155-6.

REVERDIN, O. (1945), *La Religion de la cité platonicienne* (Paris).

RHODES, P. J. (1981), *A Historical Commentary on the Aristotelian Athenaion Politeia* (Oxford).

—— (1984), 'Nomothesia in Fourth-Century Athens', *Classical Quarterly*, 35: 55-60.

RIES, G. (1989), 'Altbabylonische Beweisurteile', *Zeitschrift der Savignystiftung für Rechtsgeschichte (romisches Abteilung)*, 106: 56-80.

ROBERT, J., and ROBERT, R., (1983), *Fouilles d'Amyzon en Carie*, vol. I (Paris).

ROBERTS, J. (1982), *Accountability in Athenian Government* (Madison).

ROBERTS, S. (1979), *Order and Dispute: An Introduction to Legal Anthropology* (Harmondsworth).

ROBERTSON, N. (1990), 'The Laws of Athens, 410–399 B.C.: The Evidence for Review and Publication', *Journal of Hellenic Studies*, 110: 43–75.

ROSEN, L. (1981), 'Equity and Discretion in a Modern Islamic Legal System', *Law and Society Review*, 15/2: 217–45.

—— (1989), *The Anthropology of Justice: Law as Culture in Islamic Society*. (Cambridge).

RUDHARDT, J. (1960), 'La Définition du délit d'impiété d'après la législation attique', *Museum Helveticum*, 17: 87–105.

RUSCHE, G., and KIRCHHEIMER, O. (1939), *Punishment and Social Structure* (New York).

RUSCHENBUSCH, E. (1968), *Untersuchungen zur Geschichte des athenischen Strafrechts* (Graz).

—— (1989), review of Gagarin *Classical Philology*, 84: 342–5.

RUZÉ, F. (1988), 'Aux débuts de l'ecriture politique: Le pouvoir de l'ecrit dans la cité', pp. in Detienne (1988a), 82–94.

SAUNDERS, T. J. (1981), 'Protagoras and Plato on Punishment', 129-41 in G. B. Kerford (ed.), *The Sophists and their Legacy* (Wiesbaden), 129–41.

—— (1991), *Plato's Penal Code: Tradition, Controversy and Reform in Greek Penology* (Oxford).

SCHAPS, D. (1977), 'The Women Least Mentioned: Etiquette and Women's Names', *Classical Quarterly*, 27: 323–30.

—— (1979), *The Economic Rights of Women in Ancient Greece* (Edinburgh).

SCHULTZE, P. (1883), *De Lysias oratione trigesima* (Berlin).

SEALEY, R. (1984), 'The Tetralogies Ascribed to Antiphon', *Transactions of the American Philological Society*, 114: 71–85.

—— (1990), *Women and Law in Classical Greece* (Chapel Hill).

SHEAR, T. L. (1937), 'The Campaign of 1936', *Hesperia*, 6: 333–81.

SIMONDON, M. (1982), *La Mémoire et l'oubli dans la pensée grecque jusqu'à la fin du V^e Siecle avant J.-C.* (Paris).

SOKOLOWSKI, F. (1955), *Lois sacrées de l'Asie Mineure* (Paris).

—— (1963), *Lois sacrées des cités grecques: Supplément* (Paris).

—— (1969), *Lois sacrées des cités grecques* (Paris).

STAHL, M. (1987), *Aristokraten und Tyrannen im archaischen Athen* (Stuttgart).

STODDART, S., and WHITLEY, J., (1988), 'The Social Context of Literacy in Archaic Greece and Etruria', *Antiquity*, 62: 761–72.

STRATHERN, M. (1985), 'Discovering "Social Control"', *Journal of Law and Society*, 12: 111–34.

—— (1988), *The Gender of the Gift* (Berkeley and London).

STRATTON, J. (1980), 'Writing and the Concept of Law in Ancient Greece', *Visible Language*, 14: 99-121.

STREET, B. (1984), *Literacy in Theory and Practice* (Cambridge).

SYLLBURG, F. (1688) (ed.), Clement of Alexandria, *Stromata* (Cologne).

TALAMANCA, M. (1979), '*Dikazein e krinein* nelle testimonanze greche più antiche', in A. Biscardi (ed.), *Symposion 1974: Vorträge der griechischen und hellenistischen Rechtsgeschichte* (Cologne), 103-35.

THOMAS, C. G. (1977), 'Literacy and the Codification of Law', *Studia et Documenta Historiae et Iuris*, 43: 455-8.

THOMAS, R. (1989), *Oral Tradition and Written Record in Classical Athens* (Cambridge).

THÜR, G. (1970), 'Zum *dikazein* bei Homer', *Zeitschrift der Savigny-stiftung für Rechtsgeschichte (romisches Abteilung)*, 87: 426-44.

—— (1987), 'Formen des Urteils', in D. Simon (ed.), *Akten des 26. Deutsches Rechtshistorikertages* (Frankfurt am Main), 467-84.

—— (1989), 'Zum *dikazein* im Urteil aus Mantineau (*IG* v.2.262)', in G. Thür (ed.), *Symposion 1985. Papers on Greek and Hellenistic Legal History*. (Cologne), 55-69.

—— (1990), 'Die Todesstrafe im Blutprozess Athens', *Journal of Juristic Papyrology*, 20: 143-56.

—— (1994), 'Diskussionsbeitrag zum referat H. und M. van Effenterre', in G. Thür (ed.), *Symposiun 1993. Vorträge der griechischen und hellenistischen Rechtsgeschichte* (Cologne), 11-15.

TOD, M. N. (1948), *A Selection of Greek Historical Inscriptions*, vol. 2 (Oxford).

TODD, S. C. (1985), 'Athenian Internal Politics, 403-395 B.C., with Particular Reference to the Speeches of Lysias', Ph.D. thesis (Cambridge).

—— (1990), 'The Use and Abuse of the Attic Orators', *Greece and Rome*, 37: 159-78.

—— (1993), *The Shape of Athenian Law* (Oxford).

—— and MILLETT, P., (1990), 'Law, Society and Athens', in Cartledge *et al.* (1990), 1-18.

VALLOIS, R. (1914), '*Arai*', *Bulletin de Correspondance Hellenique*, 28: 250-71.

WEISS, E. (1923), *Griechisches Privatrecht auf rechts-vergleichender Grundlage*, vol. 1 (Leipzig).

WHITEHORNE, J. (1989), 'Punishment under the Decree of Cannonous', in G. Thür (ed.), *Symposion 1985.Vorträge der griechischen und hellenistischen Rechtsgeschichte* (Cologne), 89-97.

WILHELM, A. (1951), *Griechische Inscriften rechtlichen Inhalts*, Pragmateiai tes Akademias Athenon, 17 (Athens).

WILLETTS R.F. (1952), 'The Historical Importance of the Gortyn Laws', *University of Birmingham Historical Journal*, 3: 95-118.

—— (1954a), 'The Neotas of Gortyna', *Hermes*, 82: 494-8.

—— (1954b), 'Freedmen at Gortyna', *Classical Quarterly*, 48: 216-9.

—— (1955), *Aristocratic Society in Ancient Crete* (London).

—— (1957), 'Some Elements of Continuity in the Social Life of Ancient Crete', *International Review of Social History*, 2: 445.

—— (1958), 'Cretan Eleithyia', *Classical Quarterly*, 52: 221-3.

—— (1961a), 'Leg. Gort. I. 35-55', *Classical Quarterly*, 55: 55-60.

—— (1961b), 'διδοῖ or διδοῖ at Leg. Gort. 6.1?', *Glotta*, 39: 230-3.

—— (1961c), 'Leg. Gort. 3. 37-40', *Rheinisches Museum für Philologie*, 104: 287-8.

—— (1961d), 'On Leg. Gort. 4. 31-43', *Klio*, 39:45-7.

—— (1961e), 'καρποδαῖσται', *Philologus*, 105: 145-7.

—— (1961f), 'On Leg. Gort. 1. 15-18', *Hermes* 89: 128.

—— (1961-2), 'Cretan καδεστάς', *Kretika Chronika Proceedings of the First International Cretological Congress*, 15/16: 241-7.

—— (1962), *Cretan Cults and Festivals* (London).

—— (1963a), 'The Servile System of Ancient Crete: A Reappraisal of the Evidence', in L. Varcl and R. F. Willetts (eds.), *ΓΕΡΑΣ. Studies Presented to G. Thompson on the Occasion of his 60th Birthday* (Prague), 257-71.

—— (1963b), 'A note on Leg. Gort. 1. 2-7', *Classical Philology*, 58: 111-12.

—— (1964), 'Observations on Leg. Gort. 2. 16-20', *Kadmos*, 3: 170-6.

—— (1965a), 'ὠνεῖν = πωλεῖν', *Kadmos*, 4: 165-8.

—— (1965b), 'A Special Sense of ἐπισπένδειν', *Glotta*, 43: 251-6.

—— (1965c), 'Marriage and Kinship at Gortyn', *Proceedings of the Cambridge Philological Society*, 191: 50-61.

—— (1965d), *Ancient Crete: A Social History from Early Times until the Roman Occupation* (London).

—— (1966), 'The rights of ἐπιβάλλοντες', *Eirene*, 5: 5-16.

—— (1967), *The Law Code of Gortyn*, Kadmos suppl, 1 (Berlin).

—— (1968), 'The Date and Purpose of the Inscribing of the Gortyn Code', pp. 203-8 in *Proceedings of the Second International Cretological Congress*, vol. 2 (Athens).

—— (1972), 'The Cretan Inscription BM 1969.4-2.1: Further Provisional Comments', *Kadmos* 11:96-8.

WILLIAMSON, C. (1987), 'Monuments of Bronze: Roman Legal Documents on Bronze Tablets', *Classical Antiquity*, 6: 160-83.

WOLFF, H.J. (1946),' The Origin of Judicial Litigation among the Greeks', *Traditio*, 4: 31-87.

WORTHINGTON, I. (1994), *Persuasion. Greek Rhetoric in Action* (London).

ZIEBARTH, E. (1895), 'Der Fluch im griechischen Recht', *Hermes*, 30: 57-70.

# Index of Sources

# General Index

Lightning Source UK Ltd.
Milton Keynes UK
UKOW01n0001241216

290780UK00007B/112/P